MAN VS MONEY

Stewart Cowley has worked in the financial markets in New York and London since the 1980s. He has written columns for many of the world's leading business publications including the *Sunday Telegraph* and the financial magazine *Citywire*. He is a regular guest on BBC's *Newsnight*, Radio 4 and SKY News.

MAN VS MONEY

EVERYDAY ECONOMICS EXPLAINED

Stewart Cowley

Illustrated by Joe Lyward

Aurum
Press

First published in 2016 by Aurum Press
an imprint of The Quarto Group
The Old Brewery
6 Blundell Street
London N7 9BH
United Kingdom
www.QuartoKnows.com

This paperback edition first published in 2017 by Aurum Press

A catalogue record for this book is available from the British Library.

ISBN 978 1 78131 691 7
Ebook ISBN 978 1 78131 626 9

10 9 8 7 6 5 4 3 2 1
2021 2020 2019 2018 2017

Illustrations and design by Joe Lyward

Printed by CPI Group (UK) ltd, Croydon, CR0 4YY

'I know you think you understand what you thought I said but I'm not sure you realize that what you heard is not what I meant ...'

Alan Greenspan, Chairman of the Federal Reserve of the United States (1987–2006)

Contents

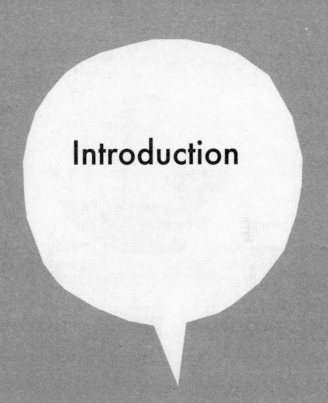

Introduction

There was a time when we were all sick and poor. About four hundred years ago the healthiest and wealthiest place in the world to live was the Netherlands. You could put it down to the cycling and the cheese but most likely it was due to the creation of the Vereenigde Oostindische Compagnie, or the Dutch East India Company.

Besides possessing a name of jaw-muscle-tightening complexity, which was the beginning of the Dutch themselves abandoning the title in their own language in favour of the much more accessible English one, the VOC was the first truly multinational corporation. It also possessed the endearing ability to wage war, print its own money and imprison and execute convicts. Annual employee assessments must have been a real hoot.

The creation of the Dutch East India Company did more than give a whole new meaning and literalism to 'being fired'; it was also the first company ever to issue shares in itself. Combined with a twenty-one-year monopoly to carry out trade activities in Asia, it made today's Apple Inc. look positively artisanal and bordering on the communist. It also gave rise to what we might like to think of as the modern economy involving companies, money and global trade.

As a consequence of this and, admittedly, other developments, global wealth and health boomed. For the next two hundred years it continued to rise from the paltry $40 a year for about forty miserable years until today, when you can expect to live a much more pleasant seventy-five years while enjoying an income of $40,000 per annum. Apart from an inconvenient dip in 1918 when the First World War conspired with a vulgar little virus called Spanish influenza to take out about 4% of the world's population, it has been a pretty much continuous and increasingly raucous global party ever since 1602.

Inevitably, our material expectations and relationship with money have changed as we have become healthier and wealthier. Money itself has changed – we have forsaken the Dutch East India Company's personally struck coinage and are now content with radio waves pinging credits between accounts or, most abstractly, have become glowingly content to accept electrons in an encoded memory board, allowing something called a virtual currency to be a means of exchange.

You would have thought that as a species we would be waving to the crowd as we pranced down the winning straight by now. But something has clearly gone very wrong with our financial system since the East India Company could strike both its own coinage and its own employees with impunity. We are now faced with a unique set of problems for the rest of the twenty-first century, some of which are due to our success, some down to simple mathematics and some that are most decidedly man-made. All of them are very real and set up an adversarial struggle with money such as we have never seen before.

The idea of this book is to shed light on some of the challenges and opportunities we have and to illustrate them for people who want to go on to learn more; hopefully this is your springboard into the depths of the subject. It is intentionally provocative – for instance, the titles of the chapters should lead you into areas you may have heard of but have not really considered before: What is bitcoin? How does a country go bust? Where is all the money? In the process we will swing from a very distant view of Planet Earth to the close-up workings of the human mind. I hope you enjoy reading the book as much as I have enjoyed writing it.

1

Economics

Is economics a fight between a dog, a cat, *Winnie-the-Pooh* and a bearded guy?

Man is in adversarial conflict with money everywhere he looks. For as long as humans have attempted to create large-scale organised societies, money and economics have been central to the attempt to create a long-lasting and stable world. But despite man's best endeavours, no economic theory has delivered anything close to a satisfactory system. And yet we keep on trying. It is the epitome of Albert Einstein's definition of madness: repeating the same behaviour over and over again and expecting a different result.

Wading through the competing ideas is equally bewildering. But to understand where we are today, you have to understand something of where we have come from. If you want to visualise it, you might characterise this as an enormous fight between a dog, a cat, some characters from *Winnie-the-Pooh* and a bearded guy.

Strikingly, all the people these characters represent have attempted to codify society through economics. They are highly intelligent and articulate and have the sole intention of making the world more understandable and ultimately better. But who were they and, given where we are today, what can we learn from them in the twenty-first century? First of all we have to have a look at who and what they thought …

The Dog – classical economics

Toby, our Cairn terrier, displays many of the characteristics of a classical economist:

- He doesn't like being told what to do: he's the same breed as the chaos-causing Toto in *The Wizard of Oz*. It's easy to sympathise with Miss Almira Gulch/the Wicked Witch of the West at times.

- The only acknowledgement he has of authority is that it is necessary for providing some basic things: opening packets of food and providing the transport to his walk each day.
- He thinks there is a mysterious unseen force, or 'hidden hand', keeping things in order. At 4.30 p.m. each day he will be sitting by his bowl, alternately staring at you and the bowl. 'Where is it?' is the clear internal question tripping across his brain. He is, frankly, bewildered as to why it isn't there but he does know, if he waits long enough, that order will be restored: food *will* appear.

Long before Toby came into this world Adam Smith published *The Wealth of Nations* in 1776 and came to pretty much the same conclusions. It marked the beginning of

classical economics. Smith realised the world was moving on from rummaging in the soil for turnips and towards a bright and shiny industrial age. Just accumulating gold wasn't enough to define wealth and the general good. What you needed was trade – if two parties exchanged goods at a profit then everyone was a winner, wealth increased and the general good prospered.

There was one big proviso, however – governments had to get out of the way of the wealth creators and let them get on with it with a minimum of meddling. The only role governments had was in providing very basic requirements such as education and these things should be paid for by those most able to pay taxes.

Adam Smith and others at the time introduced the idea that 'the market knows best'. They believed there was a self-correcting mechanism in society, the hidden hand, restoring order if things got out of line. Importantly, in one stroke Smith articulated the idea of supply and demand in a voice that is familiar today:

> *When the quantity of any commodity which is brought to market falls short of the effectual demand, all those who are willing to pay ... cannot be supplied with the quantity which they want ... Some of them will be willing to give more. A competition will begin among them, and the market price will rise ... When the quantity brought to market exceeds the effectual demand, it cannot be all sold to those who are willing to pay the whole value of the rent, wages and profit, which must be paid in order to bring it thither ... The market price will sink ...*

From that, the classicists brought into life the relationship between growth, inflation and employment in a simple set

Growth

Employment

Inflation

of observable truths. The hidden hand restored order if you waited long enough. It's a very appealing way of thinking and describing the world that has resonated for nearly three hundred years now. For it really to work, and work smoothly and efficiently, you couldn't have pesky governments or organised labour getting in the way. So if you had regulations or unions, for instance, this could slow the firing/hiring process, which should be avoided at all costs.

The other thing about the early classicists is that they had a connection with nature. They saw the functioning of the economy as that of sentient beings allocating scarce resources, which led them to have a regard for the environment. This is in stark contrast to what comes later.

The Cat – neoclassical economics

We also have a cat, called Archie. I suspect Archie is a neoclassical economist. Archie is essentially amoral in as much as he does everything for his own pleasure, cares little for the consequences of his actions on the environment and expects others to do pretty much everything for him and anticipate his every need. All this is done in near-silence. The only time you know you have got something wrong is when he 'sings the song of his people' or bites you.

Neoclassical economics also works like Archie. It is driven by a single motive: to maximise self-serving profit. It sees companies as empty vessels: stuff goes in at a cost and stuff comes out at a price to be sold. What happens inside the black box is of no interest to cat-like neoclassicists: the governance, practices, values of the institution are a mere sideshow compared to the idea that everybody is a rational business person there to make money: they see an opportunity and they go for it. This is a basic tenet of neoclassical economics and one of its weaknesses – everybody is rational despite all the evidence to the contrary.

Importantly, neoclassicists believe everybody has perfect information and companies are 'price-takers' rather than 'price-setters'. In other words, Mr Market knows best and if the world of supply and demand is out of shape, an economy will adjust very quickly to bring it back in line because out there exists an optimal equilibrium point towards which all things gravitate. That is if the world is allowed to operate efficiently with few barriers. This is the point on which both Toby and Archie would agree, and they both despise 'Big Government'.

In this group we really should include Friedrich August von Hayek if only because he and his fellow members of the Austrian School represent the far end of the neoclassical spectrum. Hayek looks a lot like the neoclassical thinkers but with one small difference – he couldn't care less about how it is working. For him even the neoclassical profit motive isn't high on the agenda. He also thought we really shouldn't meddle with society because the God of Unintended Consequences would pop up somewhere, somehow, in a way we couldn't predict. Anything you did merely set up the next problem. Best to leave it to natural forces and Darwinian natural selection. Hayek wouldn't be your first choice for a two-man assault on Everest if you were expecting trouble.

Tigger and Eeyore – John Maynard Keynes

John Maynard Keynes' economic sensibilities were forged in the First World War and its aftermath, the 1919 Versailles Peace Conference, where the fate of the newly defeated Germany was decided. Keynes was committed to the strong helping the weak: it made practical sense for economically powerful nations to come to the aid of those less fortunate. For this reason alone he saw great dangers in making Germany groan under the weight of heavy debt repayments rather than helping it rebuild its shattered economy. His words fell on deaf ears. After the Big Three (America, France and Britain) pushed through the punishment of an already enfeebled Germany, the country coped with its debts by simply turning on the printing presses. Paper money poured out so quickly you could feel the pavements around the Berlin-based Reichsbank vibrating under your feet as the presses churned. It was like putting a large-denomination note on a photocopier and placing a heavy weight on the 'Copy' button – all day. The mark collapsed, resulting in hyperinflation: prices were rising 726,000,000,000% a year by November 1923. Eventually, the Weimar Republic collapsed, paving the way for Adolf Hitler and National Socialism.

Having had a glimpse of the future, a desperately disappointed Keynes slunk back to Cambridge where he embarked upon what would become some of his best work. He made important contributions to the subject of probability which he then applied to the financial markets on his own account. He lost his shirt dealing, but it taught him something very important: financial markets and economics are inherently unpredictable. In other words, economics, markets and money are made up of irrational people who have a preference for whipping themselves up into manias and depressions, causing them to run around like a great herd of blundering toddlers for no particular reason.

Faced with this new insight, Keynes realised 'animal instinct' played a large part in explaining the world: if an economy got itself into a fug of despair a self-fulfilling downward spiral would follow. In reverse, a mania was caused by self-fulfilling overconfidence and blindness to risk. Think Eeyore, the perennially depressed donkey from A.A. Milne's *Winnie-the-Pooh*, who sees only melancholy in all situations, fighting it out with the irrepressible Tigger inside every human mind, and you pretty much have the Keynesian picture. It can only be a coincidence that *Winnie-the-Pooh* was published in 1926 when Keynes had his insights.

Combining the German experience, his beliefs of the interconnectedness of nations and his views on the irrationality of men and money only served to strengthen Keynes' belief that governments had a role to play in the economy by spending money in the bad times. He called it 'the Multiplier Effect': every pound or dollar spent by governments would reverberate around the economy many times, creating a feedback system. Confidence banished Eeyore in favour of Tigger. It may seem strange to us now but this largely fell on deaf ears for a very long time – especially in Britain. But in the 1930s Keynes found an unlikely ally in President Theodore Roosevelt, whose New Deal, a mammoth programme of public works designed to drag America out of the Great Depression, implicitly had Keynes' thumbprints all over it. You would have thought Roosevelt and Keynes had been taking long vacations together in isolated log cabins given their similarities, but when they eventually met they hated each other at first sight.

When, in 1944, they finally listened to Keynes, and were faced with the problem of creating a stable post-war global economy, the world's leaders did what any self-respecting manager does when given a difficult problem: they went to a lavish hotel in the middle of nowhere, in this case the Mount Washington Hotel, Bretton Woods, in New Hampshire. Here, the foundations for the World Bank and the International Monetary Fund were created to promote the idea of interconnectedness and to end economic nationalism, something Keynes felt so strongly about.

It was only after the Second World War that Keynesian-style government spending really took off. Sadly, Keynes died suddenly in 1946 of a heart attack at the age of just sixty-two. He didn't get to see how his ideas would dominate a generation until, in the 1970s, they were abandoned for free-market ideologies.

The Bearded Guy – Karl Marx

Classical economics and liberal thinkers in the eighteenth and nineteenth centuries were united on at least one point: of the three definable stations in society – workers, landlords and capitalists – the last people you should give money to was the workers. The reasoning was simple: if you give money to workers they will fritter it away on gin, the music hall and, if they had been invented then, games consoles.

If you give money to capitalists their involuntary reflex is to invest it and make more money out of it. This idea (the way to long-term, sustainable wealth creation) avoided today's consumption and increased investment. This idea was laid bare in *The Communist Manifesto*, written in 1848 by Karl Marx and Friedrich Engels. Their view was that such delayed gratification allowed the owners of property to exploit those without property even if everybody got to live in a nicer house.

Importantly, Marx and Engels spotted that capitalism, as envisaged by the classicist, had an inherent set of contradictions inside of it making it 'its own grave digger'. Marx realised the consistent transfer of wealth into the hands of the few would leave the toiling factory workers with no money to buy the goods on offer. In order to fill the gap between what you earn and what you want, people would

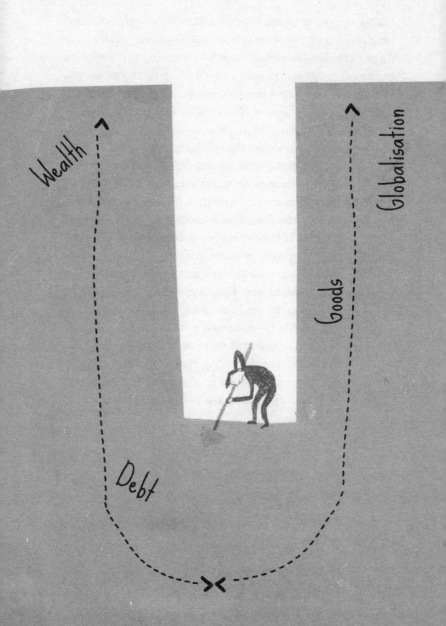

borrow money. At the same time capitalists, who are only driven by a lascivious desire for profit, would gamble and borrow money in order to create production to pay for what they borrowed. If the borrowing loop stopped, the whole edifice collapsed.

So for capitalism to work it had to have a functioning banking system and, unless it was properly managed, debts would build up to a catastrophic level, which would in turn lead to capitalism's own destruction. For Marx and Engels it was inevitable: all you had to do was sit back and wait, and even if today's crisis wasn't 'the Big One', not to worry: a bigger one would be along in a minute such was capitalism's debt addiction.

Strangely, Marx and Engels weren't wholly against capitalism; they saw many virtues in it, especially in being able to deliver globalisation and bring goods and services to ordinary people where they had only been available to a privileged few. But despite this, Marx concluded the workers were being inexcusably exploited and should unite in revolution and seize the means of production. Hence 'Workers of the World Unite!!!', the final words of the manifesto.

Man vs Economics

All these theories are born of personal experience in their time. Keynes was scarred by the First World War and German hyperinflation following the Treaty of Versailles. Karl Marx was energised by the inequalities of the industrial age in Germany and Victorian Britain. The neoclassicists were a reaction against government expenditure and union power in the post-war period. Each theory has the ring of truth about it but ultimately lacked the universality of a physical law applicable in all points in space, all of the time. What's more, whatever we do in economics appears to be almost exactly wrong but for the briefest periods of time, which is where Hayek is more than probably right: we are always one step behind what is needed. If economists were musicians they'd be big fans of syncopation.

The credit crunch of 2008 robbed us of yet another modish certainty: Mr Market knows best. Bailing out the system using government money, just as the neoclassicists said wasn't needed, was like picking up the drunken teenager from the school prom – they thought they knew it all but they realised they needed Mummy and Daddy when they got into trouble.

Now we sit at a fork in the road, or what you might call the point where the bowl meets the stem of *the Martini Glass of Existence*. One direction takes us towards Keynes

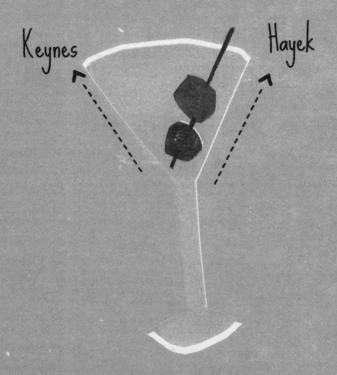

Keynes   Hayek

and the other towards Hayek. The struggle is now between those two ideas – roughly where the olive is. But western economies don't have the money to apply Keynesian cures any more – we have built up too many debts at a national and personal level – while allowing free rein to the markets appears to be foolish. Self-restraint seems completely beyond us, leading to ever larger booms and ever larger busts, just as Marx predicted. However, what is striking is that, for all its faults, capitalism has won and still flourishes – somehow. The fall of the Berlin Wall, the collapse of Soviet Russia and the gradual transformation of China into a free-market economy all illustrate that, for all its faults, its periodic bust-ups and excesses, the dominant force in economics in the twenty-first century will most likely be capitalism.

All economic theories are born of personal experience

...

so what wins?

2

Statistics

Do pandas calculate
economic statistics?

Statistics are so monumentally unreliable they can get you killed, especially if you are a panda. China, which is home to all the world's wild pandas, held its fourth National Giant Panda Survey in 2015, at which it announced that there are now 1,864 giant pandas living in the Sichuan, Shaanxi and Gansu provinces compared to 1,596 in 2003 – in other words, the giant wild panda population has risen 17% in just over a decade.

This is a remarkable result for the dopily unassuming and endearing Chinese giant panda. Being, in equal measure, squeamish about physical contact and almost unable to digest their sole source of nutrition – bamboo – isn't a great combination. Not so long ago there was a very real danger they would die out altogether.

Now, their rapid rate of population growth threatens to outstrip their delicate ecosystem. On the face of it, just looking at the statistics, they should be reclassified from 'endangered', requiring lavish research facilities with enclosures featuring discreet, sensuous mood music to encourage intimacy, to 'pest', requiring a carefully controlled culling programme.

Characteristically, the full panda data was not released nor was it explained how China came to such suspiciously accurate numbers – 1,864 is pretty specific. Taken together, opacity and specificity ought to set alarm bells ringing in any enquiring mind.

We have a similar relationship with economic statistics: we turn a blind eye to what they are or even how they are arrived at. There is a kind of assumption of their authority and scientific accuracy that is simultaneously comforting but is looking increasingly questionable. At the same time some of the old certainties are beginning to dissolve. There is a real question mark around the fitness for purpose of the economic numbers that people, businesses and policy-setters scrutinise most closely to base their decisions on in the twenty-first century. To illustrate this we are going to look at just one of the most widely used numbers – overall economic growth – to understand why they have become a poor way of making our judgements.

That's really gross ...

The gross domestic product (GDP) of a country is an important number; it measures the value of all the things sold, which in turn tells you something about overall economic health. GDP numbers are announced regularly, usually every three months starting in March. Markets, the media and politicians fetishise over them to an alarming degree. Among other things, it gives them a steer on whether companies are doing well or whether interest rates and economic policy should be adjusted.

The problem with economic numbers like GDP (and I don't mean to pick on GDP – there are certainly others) is they are, by and large, taking all the factors into account and seeing things from both sides – a terrible way of making decisions in your life. To understand why we must look at what GDP is.

In its simplest form gross domestic product is everything sold in an economy at its final price (i.e. how you see it in the shops rather than halfway through being made). Sometimes people will also talk about GDP as a measure of the income of an economy: for every buyer there is a seller, which says something about what we are consuming. So in its crudest form:

Gross Domestic Product = National Income.

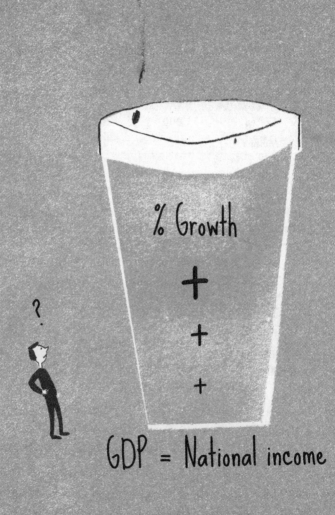

% Growth

+

+

+

GDP = National income

On the face of it GDP is easy to calculate. Let's use an example. Since we live in a café society let's invent a nation whose entire economic activity consists of selling coffee and muffins while updating their profile on Facebook, which isn't so very different from large areas of western civilisation these days. The GDP of Coffeeworld consists of counting the number of cups of coffee and muffins sold and their prices. Multiplying them together gives you Coffeeworld's GDP.

	Number	Price	Total
Coffee	1,000	3.50	3,500
Muffins	400	1.50	600
Total			4,100

Coffeeworld has a GDP consisting exclusively of $4,100 worth of coffee and muffins. Now let's roll things forward a year and see what has happened in the economy.

	Year 1			Year 2		
	Number	Price	Total	Number	Price	Total
Coffee	1,000	3.50	3,500	1,200	4.00	4,800
Muffins	400	1.50	600	600	2.00	1,200
Total			4,100			6,000

In year two the GDP of our caffeine-based society rose from $4,100 to $6,000 in one year. To put it into percentage increase terms:

$$percentage\ change\ =\ \frac{final-Initial}{Initial} \times 100$$

Which in our case is:

$$percentage\ change\ =\ \frac{6{,}000-4{,}100}{4100} \times 100$$

$$percentage\ change = 46\%$$

If you lived in Coffeeworld and you were watching the news this evening, you would hear the following. *First up – GDP rises 46% this year. President Cowley announces plans for twenty-four-hour danceathon to work off that caffeine and get you "Beach Ready" ...'* You might expect everyone to be excited by this. And so they are, except for one group: economists …

Get real!!!

Forty-six per cent sounds like a phenomenal number and it is: it would be enough to give your average coffee franchise owner a feeling of juddering ecstasy. Most economies grow around 2 to 3% a year (if they are lucky). In Coffeeworld this massive rise in activity could be explained by caffeine and sugar-based hyperactivity but the truth is more mundane. If you look at the differences between 2015 and 2016 you will see two things are happening. First, the number of cups of coffee and muffins are increasing but *also* their price is changing. Rising prices are referred to as 'inflation'. So the growth rate of 46% is a result of both price and quantity changing. Alternatively, the prices and quantity might be staying the same and the size of your cup of coffee getting bigger, but that almost never happens.

This annoys economists: it doesn't tell them what is going on in the underlying economy. All the growth counted this way could be due to prices alone increasing, which doesn't tell you very much – it's a bit unreal.

This is why most people like to talk about 'nominal' and 'real' GDP. What we calculated first time around is known as 'nominal GDP'. Real (as opposed to, say, 'imaginary') GDP is calculated by keeping the prices the same, using some date in the past as your starting point or baseline, and counting up the number of units sold and doing the calculation again, like this:

	Year 1			Year 2		
	Number	Price	Total	Number	Price	Total
Coffee	1,000	3.50	3,500	1,200	3.50	4,200
Muffins	400	1.50	600	600	1.50	900
Total			4,100			5,100

So now in our example you will notice the price columns haven't changed and our real GDP number is now $5,100. Plug this into our percentage change equation and we find real GDP increased by 24% rather than the 46% for nominal GDP. We have stripped out the effect of the price of the coffee/muffin combo going up (usually the case) or going down (rarely the case) to reveal the true or real growth rate of our economy. Economists can now join in the celebrations but perhaps you should avert your eyes from their dancing.

The good, the bad and the downright ugly...

There is something important to notice about GDP calculations. First of all, GDP statistics, by their nature, make no distinction between 'good' and 'bad' economic activity. For instance, it's been estimated that the 1995 trial of the former American football star O.J. Simpson for the murder of his wife and her friend added some $200 million to US GDP through legal fees, hotel costs and TV coverage. Although lots of job-creating goods and services were sold, this should not be taken as advocating a society where sensationalist murder trials are its main economic activity.

Another shortcoming of GDP calculations is that they deal with the average of all activity or the average person. They make no allowance for inequality of the distribution of income: you could have a very large number of people earning or consuming a small amount and very few people earning a very large amount and you wouldn't be able to tell whether you had a healthy economy or not. In the past fifteen years, an unequal distribution of income and wealth has grown in many developed societies, making GDP as a guide to policy-making less and less useful as time has gone on. What was useful even twenty years ago is now a questionable yardstick by which to judge a society.

GDP also only measures activity you can put a price upon. It doesn't measure things not involving a transaction. So, for instance, the work of those who stay at home to look after children or the childcare offered by grandparents isn't valued. Equally, in society today we have tended towards self-employment and short-term contracts which can often lead to work being done that isn't fully valued – lots of 'free work' is being done as a loss leader or in order to secure contracts because of the insecurity of tenure. Free work in society

How do you measure things?

What's the price of coffee?

What's the value of ecology?

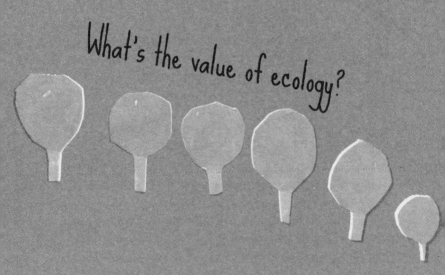

simply doesn't show up in GDP even though it is crucial to its operation.

Equally worrying is the absence of any allowance for the environmental impact of economic activity. For instance, in our fictitious coffee-centric world we could be cutting down forests to enable the further growth and supply of coffee beans and wheat for muffins. If Coffeeworld were a small island, very soon all the forests would be gone. The situation would be unsustainable and yet up to the moment the last surviving member of society sipped their last cup of coffee while pressing the 'Like' button on a photograph of a kitten on their Smartphone, GDP would have continued to grow and all would have looked well according to the accountants. Some economists argue we should account for resource depletion and use so-called 'green GDP' incorporating the idea of sustainability. Marc and Marque-Luisa Miringoff ingeniously came up with the *genuine progress indicator* (GPI) which sought to incorporate the impact of environmental and social factors into GDP. Disturbingly, they found the GPI steadily rose from 1950 until the 1970s but has been tailing off ever since. Meanwhile, traditional GDP showed an unbroken upward trend. It should come as no surprise that the oil and coal industries aren't overly keen on adopting GPI as a measure of economic activity because of its focus on environmental factors.

Still the calculation of GDP is mesmerisingly powerful mainly because the way it is worked out is so magically plausible. In Coffeeworld we only looked at the sale of coffee and muffins. But for an entire modern country it's a bit more complicated than that. The principles, however, remain the same. For a country the elements of GDP are:

$$GDP = (C)onsumption + (G)overnment\ Expenditure +$$
$$(I)nvestment + Net\ e(X)ports$$

Each one of these moving parts has to be calculated somewhere and by someone, often in nation-defining detail. For instance, in the US the number one list-topping category is motor vehicles and parts. If you dig into the numbers you will find Americans spend about five times more on tyres alone than they do on providing meals in elementary schools.

But how is this fine detail gathered? They guess. That's right, they guess a lot of the time because:

a) the data isn't available,
b) it isn't very accurate when it is available, and
c) the available data doesn't quite fit into the correct GDP categories.

In the case of GDP this leads to something euphemistically called 'the statistical discrepancy'. To give you an idea how large the statistical discrepancy can be, in the first three months of 2011 the US economy was 'missing' about $180,000,000,000 ($180 billion if that helps), which was about 1.2% of GDP at the time. This is pretty much the *entire* estimated quarterly growth. Later it was found down the back of the sofa in a coffee room.

In very large societies fine measurement of all activity is understandably difficult but it becomes a problem when your policy setters are placing so much emphasis on it to make decisions. It's also a real problem when one of the most important nations in the world just doesn't play the GDP game. The most unrepentantly inaccurate GDP calculating country of all, by its own admission, is China. To their credit Chinese statisticians don't even pretend their GDP numbers are worth the paper they are written on. Former premier Zhu Rongji even wondered out loud how it could be that all five Chinese provinces could grow faster than the country as a whole while Li Keqiang, who became premier in 2013, dismissed the numbers as 'man-made'. This is unnerving given that China is set to become the largest economy in the world in the next decade. They also usually turn up two days after the end of a quarter, which is suspiciously impressive for a country of China's size and complexity. Maybe they have the excess pandas working on it.

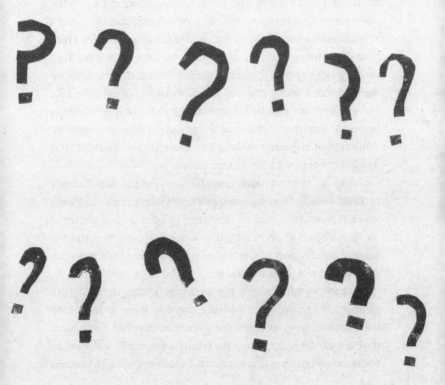

Man vs Economic Statistics

Whether you are a person or a business, there is a real and increasing problem basing important life decisions on reported GDP numbers: they don't tell us much about what real people are doing, what the real effect it has on the environment or the general health of society, and they aren't very accurate. Layer on top the fact that China, whose current economic trajectory sees it set to dominate the twenty-first century, doesn't care for accurate economic statistics, what we thought was a useful and cosy certainty is becoming decidedly fuzzy. This may just be an understandable clash of cultures between western Socratic and eastern Confucian ways of thinking but it doesn't make it any less real nor should it stop us openly acknowledging its existence.

And it doesn't really end there. Twenty-first-century problems such as rising inequality, environmental concerns and a lack of relevance to what real people do is something we haven't had to contend with on this scale before. And yet we still set economic and social polices using indicators of doubtful relevance and accuracy.

It's important that people start questioning the authority given to these numbers because there is good evidence to show that how we account for society affects our behaviour: if you measure success in a particular way people will tend to focus on optimising that measure. In other words, if policies are focused upon only increasing GDP with no regard to its consequences then that is how people and companies will act. As we'll see later, our increased interconnectedness and relationship with the things that have made human beings so economically successful is starting to become somewhat strained. It follows that, in the remainder of the twenty-first century, we may have to be more aware of how we judge 'success' and start rethinking the economic statistics that guide our actions.

3

Compound interest

Should I buy a house
using a credit card?

We all borrow money at some point in our lives. It might start with the occasional and fleeting overdraft, develop into a credit card, escalate into a loan for a car and before you know it you are hooked on mortgage payments. And yet even though we are told the words, we rarely listen to what we are charged as an interest rate.

In 1987 I did something really stupid mainly because I didn't understand what interest rates could do to a person. I bought a house using a credit card.

That's right. When UK interest rates were 15% a year and credit card rates were 25% and more I put a deposit of £5,000 down on our first home using a credit card.

It's difficult to explain to people these days what a giddy sensation suddenly having access to credit was like. It was the nitrous oxide at the money rave. The idea that you could have pretty much anything you wanted whenever you wanted it, as long as you didn't think about or even know about the consequences, was a new sensation for many. And that was only the beginning of a global phenomenon. The result has been a pretty much unbroken thirty-year run of increasing debts for everyone, especially in the West.

At the same time interest rates have, in general, fallen. We've experienced exceptionally low interest rates since the banking crisis of 2008. This has helped borrowers keep their payments manageable while savers have seen negligible returns on their money, for most of the time below inflation. Every day the real value of their savings has decreased.

This phenomenon of high debts and low interest rates is something some would say we have become habituated to and, like hostages, we have begun to identify with our captors – we sort of think of it as normal. When was the last time you heard someone say they couldn't come out that night because they were saving up for a fridge? Probably never. Instant gratification is the order of the day.

As things stand interest rates on credit cards are now roughly what mortgage rates were back in 1987. So if I was willing to buy a house then with a mortgage rate of 15% why shouldn't I buy a house using a credit card today? The answer lies in understanding what interest rates are and what they can do to you as a borrower or a saver, especially in a world where access to credit has never been easier.

Very interesting rates

The two most commonly advertised rates are the yearly interest rate per annum (PA), and an annual percentage rate, or APR. There is a big difference between these two rates but not many people know what it is. People's ignorance of this has turned it into a multi-billion-dollar business. At the paramilitary end of the spectrum it is the short term or payday loans market that is so extreme it makes a great way of illustrating the difference.

We have begun to
identify with our
captors – we think
it's normal.

Payday loan companies put out advertisements for interest rates of 292% PA, which is 1,499.3% APR (I'm not kidding; they will actually include the 0.3% at the end). The reason for the difference is there are administration costs in there somewhere. No matter how much they scream and shout there aren't, there really are. It's the first warning sign. This is how it works.

Let's take the example of someone borrowing $100 for thirteen days. The interest rate is 0.8% or 80¢ a day. So, after thirteen days you will have to repay interest of $13 \times 80¢ = 10.40 plus the initial loan of $100. The annual interest rate is $0.8\% \times 365 = 292\%$, just like in the advertisement.

But, what if there is an administration fee of $43 just for doing the work of arranging the loan? Now your total cost of borrowing is $53.40, requiring a total repayment of $153.40 after just thirteen days. Annualise it, which is $365 \times \frac{53.4}{13}$, and you realise that the true APR is actually 1,499.3%, all because of the administration fees. Administration fees won't change no matter how long you borrow for and the shorter the time over which you borrow the higher the APR becomes. This trick can apply to a range of loans – credit cards, mortgages, you name it. If you ever see the letters PA and APR in an advertisement start asking questions.

The other thing to look out for is the word 'representative'. You'll hear and read this a lot in financial advertising. What it actually translates into is 'for most people but not necessarily you'. The word 'typical' is also used, which is sort of typical of them. So, once again, what you see might not be what you get.

It's no less confusing if you are a depositor and have money in an interest-bearing account. You will often see the words 'annual equivalent rate' (AER) and 'gross' applied to savings rate. Let's put $1,000 in an account and leave it there at a gross rate of 3%. At the end of the year you will have $1,030, which you will receive if you leave it there.

Now let's imagine you get paid the interest monthly or 3% / 12 = 0.25% per month. After one month you will have $1,002.50 in your account. Now you have to apply the monthly rate not to $1,000 but to your $1,002.50, which means you will receive your monthly interest and also interest on your interest. This is called 'compound interest'. At the end of month two you will have $1,005.01, which is slightly more than just doubling one month's interest. Keep doing this and at the end of twelve months you will have about $1,030.42 which is $0.42 difference from the gross amount. So you actually have two different interest rates: 3% gross or 3.042 % AER, depending upon when you receive the interest.

This might not seem a big difference but when you do it over millions or billions of savings it really adds up. But as a rule of thumb the AER will always be above the gross amount. In other words when comparing potential savings accounts always compare like for like.

If you wanted to write out what we have just done, over the first couple of months it would look like this:

$$1,000 \times (1.0025) \times (1.0025) = 1,005.01,$$ which isn't so bad.

But by month twelve it looks like this:

$$1,000 \times (1.0025) \times (1.0025) \times$$
$$(1.0025) \times (1.0025) \times (1.0025) \times$$
$$(1.0025) \times (1.0025) \times (1.0025) \times$$
$$(1.0025) \times (1.0025) \times (1.0025) \times$$
$$(1.0025) = 1,030.42,$$ which if it were to go on any longer would start to test your patience. Which leads us to …

Confounding compounding

Albert Einstein relegated his $E = MC^2$ equation to a footnote in history; when asked what he considered man's greatest invention he is alleged to have replied, somewhat playfully,

'Compound interest.'

The equation for compound interest looks like this:

$$FV = PV\ (1+\tfrac{r}{n})^{nt}$$

It doesn't look much but it is mind-bogglingly powerful. What it is saying is the future value (FV) of something is whatever it is worth today, the present value (PV), multiplied by the interest rate repeated by the number of times it goes on for.

So let's take our example of monthly interest of 5% PA over one year:

Present value = $1,000, r = 3%, n = 12 (months), t = 1 (year).

Plug this into the equation and you get:

$$FV = \$1,000 \times (1 + 0.03/12)^{(12 \times 1)}$$

$$FV = \$1,000 \times (1.0025)^{12}$$

$$FV = \$1,030.42$$

This is exactly the same answer as before. All the heavy lifting has been done for you. It's quite amazing. The really neat part of it is the $(\ )^{12}$, or 'power of 12' part, which most handheld calculators or calculator apps can do.

Savings or debt, it's all
a matter of compound interest.

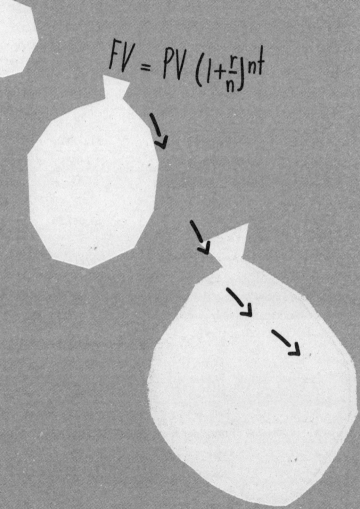

$$FV = PV \left(1 + \frac{r}{n}\right)^{nt}$$

If you were to look at what happens over two years, replacing the 12 with 24 (2 years × 12 months), then you would have $1,061.76 all because you are now receiving interest and interest on interest. When you realise what is going on here you could be forgiven for the miserly look that suddenly appears on your face. Interest on top of interest is literally money for nothing.

The infinite possibilities of compound interest should now be appearing to you. But to be honest, after a while even with a calculator, going through the routine loses the thrill of the first blush of familiarity. But not to worry, help is at hand. You can write a spreadsheet to do it for you. And here it is.

	A	B
1	PV	$1,000.00
2	Rate	3.00%
3	Number of Times per Year	12
4	Years	2
5	FV	$1,061.76

The little hat symbol ^ in the following spreadsheet cells means 'to the power of' and does the compounding for you. All you have to do now is plug the numbers in and it will do all the work of calculating your one, which should give you hours of fun – but don't tell anybody.

	A	B
1	PV	1000
2	Rate	0.03
3	Number of Times per Year	12
4	Years	2
5	FV	=B1*(1+B2/B3)^(B3*B4)

For instance, you can start asking some real questions about the interest rate you are receiving on your savings and what it means to you over the next couple of years – all you have to do is plug the numbers into the spreadsheet and it will tell you the answer. This could be especially useful if you want to save up for a specific amount. If you have $2,000 and you need $2,500 in two years' time, what would the interest rate need to be for you to achieve your goal? By plugging $2,000 into 'PV', 12 into 'Number of Times per Year', 2 in 'Years' and changing the 'Rate', you'd find you'd need an account which gives you 11.2%. If you aren't getting 11.2% at your bank then it's time to look around for a higher rate or conclude that you have to put some more money away.

On the flip side, if you are the interest payer then your simple debt is going to be much bigger than you originally thought. To ram this home let's see what happens if you borrow $100 for longer than a few days from a payday loan company at 1,500%, which isn't unusual. Plug it into the equation and you will find that, in less than two years, you would owe $35 trillion, which is more than all the government debt in the world. They'd probably want the $43 administration fee as well.

In October 1987 something calamitous happened – 10% of the value of global stock markets was vaporised in the course of a single working day and with it a huge number of jobs, including mine. The £5,000 credit card payment for my deposit was suddenly an impressive debt that wasn't going away. If I had used the compound interest calculation then I could have plugged the numbers in and found in just five years I would owe over £17,000 – every day hurts a little bit more.

This is the power of compounding. It's the repetition doing the damage. As an individual or a country borrowing money you really shouldn't mess with compound interest.

Man vs Compound Interest

Nobody knows where interest rates will go in the future – we are told the twenty-first-century's 'new normal' is for continuous very low interest rates, but we do know there is an awful lot of debt in society. Individuals, companies and governments have raised borrowing to unprecedented levels in the past thirty years, leaving many people extraordinarily sensitive to even small interest rate changes and the effects of compound interest.

For savers the lessons from compound interest teach you another thing: consistent interest and the passage of time is your friend. As long as inflation is below the interest rate on your savings, the real value of your money will be growing at an ever-increasing rate all because of compounding, especially if you start saving early enough. The sooner you start the better it is at the end.

What sometimes gets in the way of this fundamental truth – start early and leave it alone – is that there is the huge temptation in twenty-first-century finance to switch investments around. In fact it has never been easier, as we'll see later. It is now easy to buy and sell investments on a mobile phone via an app. What's more, investors are positively encouraged to do so. From time to time there may be a good reason to do this but only in extreme cases. In general it's something you should resist doing because what has not changed and never will change is that, given sufficient time and a consistent rate of return on your money, you will become wealthier day by day, and the reason for that is compound interest.

4

Bonds

Is the biggest threat to your wealth your safest investment?

Karl Marx understood that for capitalism to work it needed a functioning financial system lending money to buy things you couldn't afford. It also meant capitalism was doomed to periodic crises – each one ever larger – because capitalism was apt to take a good idea too far from time to time. It just couldn't help itself, he concluded.

Most people imagine the place you borrow money from is a bank. In fact the place where the really big money changes hands is the bond markets. The bond markets are enormous. They dwarf the size of the stock markets many times over. In 2015 the total size of the US government bond market was nearly $40 trillion, which is about twice the value of America's top five hundred companies. Globally, the top twenty-five developed nations alone have government debts of over $33 trillion and it's rising every day – and every penny of it is borrowed via the bond market. It really is staggering and yet you seldom hear mention of the bond markets in mainstream media.

You could say the bond markets are the worst kept secret everybody has heard of. I say 'secret' because everybody will have heard of government borrowing but not many people know how it happens, care even less about how it works and where the bonds end up or understand there is an enormous industry out there trading them. On average a staggering $1 trillion of global bonds are traded each day. And there is a lot of money to be made trading bonds: don't forget that Jay Gatsby's gothic mansion in West Egg in *The Great Gatsby* was bought with the proceeds of bond trading.

Since the turn of the millennium interest rates have declined to astonishingly low levels. Combined with an ageing population, which tends to live off the income of a lifetime's savings, there is now a collision between the need for income and what's available. Logically, savers and pensioners have been tempted to take money out of bank deposits and look for alternative and higher sources of income and that means the bond markets.

To be frank, the bond markets are boring. They are constructed to be the most tedious and safe places to put your money. But now the bond markets come with risks people are simply unaware of, which comes from a surprising source – mathematics – and are governed by four rules which few people know about.

The name's bond, financial bond ...

Putting your money on deposit is all very well and your returns are governed by the equation for compound interest:

$$FV = PV \left(1 + \frac{r}{n}\right)^{nt}$$

The accumulation of interest and interest upon interest is a powerful thing, as we saw in the previous chapter. There is a rearrangement of the compound interest equation that's really important – it has brought down nations and destroyed high-flying business careers. And it's this:

$$PV = \frac{FV}{\left(1 + \frac{r}{n}\right)^{nt}}$$

It might not look like very much but what it is saying is 'How much do I have to put down *today* to get a fixed amount in the future based on today's interest rate?' The PV (present value) is just the price of the future fixed payment. The 'r' is the market rate, or yield, today and 'nt' is the maturity date – the

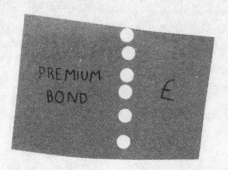

day when you get all the money back you originally lent. In other words we have just invented the global bond markets.

When bonds first came into existence they were literally a piece of paper like a bank note. Down the side of them was a series of detachable pieces of paper that investors could hand in and get their interest payment on the day it was due. Interest payments on bonds became known as 'coupons' and the name has stuck even to this day.

The most common form of coupons are paid twice a year (semi-annual) or once a year (annual). But to keep things simple, let's just imagine that the bond pays once a year. The present value or price of the bond is just the money you put down to receive the expected fixed coupon payments and get your money back at the end. So a bond paying 5% semi-annually for, say, one year would be worth $105 for every $100 you put down when market yields are 5%. Plug those numbers into our equation and you get this:

$$FV = 105, r = 5\%, n = 1, t = 1$$

$$Price = PV = 105/(1 + 0.05)^{(1 \times 1)}$$

$$Price = PV = \$100$$

Now let's change things. Imagine your central bank *increases* interest rates to 7% just after you bought the 5% bond and market rates have risen accordingly. If you wanted to sell your 5% bond nobody would want to buy it at $100 because now they could get 7% out in the market. You now have to adjust the price of the bond down to compensate for the new market rate. So what is the price (PV) of your bond? Our equation does the work for us:

$$Price = PV = 105/(1 + 0.07)^1$$

$$Price = PV = 98.13$$

If you were to sell now, it would only be worth $98.13 to the buyer. If you were forced to sell today you would make a loss.

Now let's reverse the situation. Let's imagine some terrible economic news has been announced and your local central bank *reduces* interest rates to 3%. You own something paying a rate higher than is on offer in the market. If you were to sell it the buyer would have to compensate you with a price higher than the original $100. What is the bond worth now?

$$Price = PV = 105/(1 + 0.03)^1$$

$$Price = PV = 101.94$$

The price of the bond has risen by $1.94 to reflect the fact that the fixed coupon rate is higher than what's available in the market. You could now sell the bond and make a profit.

The new market rate is called the 'yield' and the process we have been through is the opposite of compounding and is called 'discounting'. But the main thing to notice is, using bonds, you can buy and hold a bond to maturity or you can trade the interest rate markets, guessing the direction of interest rates, and make money.

It's a weird idea and takes some time to get your head around – but it's true. If you think interest rates are going to fall in the future, then you could buy bonds at today's rates and watch the price rise as it happens. Or if you thought interest rates were going to rise, you should sell your bonds, watch the price fall then reinvest when you think yields are at the right level and are set to fall again. This is the essence of bond trading.

Even if you don't get the mathematics here are the rules:

> *Rule 1 As yields fall bond prices rise*

> *Rule 2 As yields rise bond prices fall*

This is very important. Fortunes can be won and lost knowing it. But it gets better because there is another rule which comes from the mathematics of bonds and it's this:

> *Rule 3 The longer the maturity of a bond, the more its price moves when yields change*

Just to show how powerful an effect this can be, imagine you bought, not a one-year maturity bond, but one maturing in thirty years with a 5% coupon and yields fell from 5 to 3%. The price of the bond would rise from $100 to just over $139 – or a 39% return from the price alone. If yields rose to 7% the price of the bond would fall to nearly $75, which is a loss of 25% on your original investment.

So if you can anticipate the movements of yields you could make (or lose) money by trading in and out of bonds as yields rise and fall. You would maximise your return by purchasing long-maturity bonds as yields fell or protect yourself by selling into cash or buying short-maturity bonds as yields rise. These rules don't come from any ideology, don't rely upon complicated sociological observations and they certainly aren't subject to political intervention – they are a function of mathematics. All you have to do is correctly guess the future direction of interest rates and bond yields.

Returnless risk

There is one thing about bonds we have not discussed yet and again it's to do with mathematics. Rather than go through why this is, it's enough to understand another rule about how their prices move and it's this:

> Rule 4 *The lower the yield the larger the price movement when yields change.*

This is an enormously important idea because of where we are today. Long before the 2008 credit crunch the world was on a journey to lower and lower interest rates and bond yields. Globalisation, increased competition, technology, the decline in global inflation, the emergence of China – all have been cited as reasons. From the mid-1990s bond yields in general declined by one third (see following graph) from about 6% to about 4% across the bond markets.

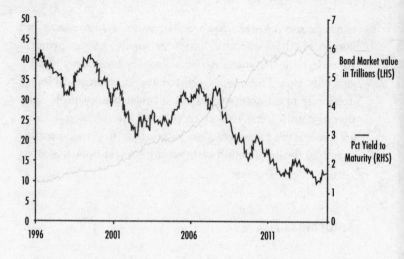

Bond Market value in Trillions (LHS)

Pct Yield to Maturity (RHS)

And then the credit crunch hit in 2008. One of the things everybody eventually agreed upon was the need to keep interest rates down so the world wouldn't go bust and borrowing could start again to revive the economy.

Short-term interest rates were slashed to zero while central banks began the policy known as quantitative easing (QE) intended to drive down long-term borrowing rates. If you were a saver you were positively encouraged to take your money out of the bank and grab the higher income from the bond market – while they lasted. Globally, money flooded into bond mutual funds. It was a rational response in an irrational world.

In just over six years the bond markets rose in size by 50% – everybody did what they were supposed to do and borrowed money literally like there was no tomorrow. One measure of the size of the bond market rose in value by $15 trillion in the space of just six years. It had taken nearly a decade to achieve the same thing and the most remarkable thing about it was that it was done in the teeth of the greatest financial crisis seen for a generation. It was staggeringly impressive.

As yields were driven down and investors were driven into the bond markets because their income had all but evaporated, Rule 4 kicked in; what was supposed to be the boring and safe investment in your savings had been turned into something incredibly risky. If bond yields rose at any point in the future, prices would plummet in a way never seen before and it is entirely due to the mathematics of bonds.

To give you a feel for this let's imagine a thirty-year maturity bond yielding 2%. If yields rose to 4% then the price would drop to about $65, which is a 35% loss. Compare it to the example when the starting yield was 5%. An identical 2% rise in yields causes a 25% loss, which is still big but it proves the lower the starting point when yields rise the bigger the loss. What was supposed to be your most tedious investment just became exciting but not in a good way.

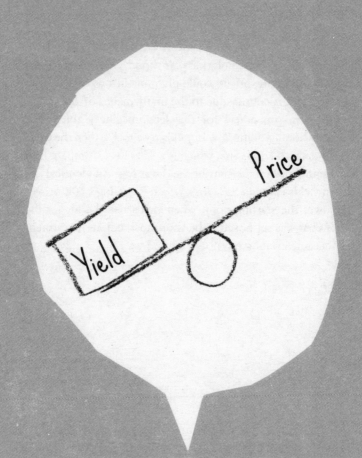

Man vs Bonds

The world is stuffed with bonds. If you have a workplace pension fund then there are bonds in it. If you have a regular savings product with the word 'balanced' or 'target return' in it then there are bonds in it. Goodness, even the bank you have your money in has bonds in it – their reserves they lay aside for a rainy day, when there are people hammering on the windows demanding their money back, are kept in bonds.

Independently of this the general public has a chance of playing the interest rate markets and they do. The most convenient way to get exposure to the bond markets is through collective schemes: mutual funds in the United States, Open-Ended Investment Companies (OEICs) in the UK. More widely throughout Europe people get access to the bond markets via the snappily named Undertakings for Collective Investments in Transferable Securities, better known as UCITS funds, or SICAVs, which is an abbreviation of Société d'Investissement À Capital Variable. No matter the name the intention is the same: to allow investors to pool their money into funds that they can buy and sell on a daily basis. To give you an idea of the numbers, between 2005 and 2014 more than $2 trillion flowed into bond funds alone. The wealth of investors across the world is heavily exposed to the bond markets and their price movements.

If trying to predict the future is foolhardy, predicting that nothing will change in the future is equally unrealistic: nobody knows the precise path of interest rates or bond yields in the future. But we do know they can't stay low or keep on falling forever. So, as a starting point for bond investing the early twenty-first century wouldn't be the place you would choose. Our Four Rules of Bond Investing,

> *Rule 1 As yields fall bond prices rise*
> *Rule 2 As yields rise bond prices fall*
> *Rule 3 The longer the maturity of a bond, the more its price moves when yields change*
> *Rule 4 The lower the yield the larger the price movement when yields change*

make it all but inevitable that, at some point, bond markets are going to experience a reversal of fortunes like nothing we have seen before and all because the mathematics of bonds. Rules 2, 3 and 4 are what make the situation uniquely dangerous. If an investor is exposed to long-dated bonds at today's yield levels, and yields begin to rise, they are in trouble – prices are going to fall and then some.

This is a bizarre coincidence. Just at the time when our population is ageing and savers are looking to move from accumulating wealth to protecting what they have, while needing a regular income from their savings at retirement, your money has never been more exposed to risk. This comes in two forms: the risk that your savings are eroded by inflation as you could become locked into an interest rate lower than the rate prices are rising, and more importantly, the risk of potential capital losses from bonds that experience the kind of price movements you might expect from a high-risk equity investment.

BONDS:
A pool for investors to buy and sell on a daily basis

5

Banks

Breakfast doesn't count ...

It might sound obvious but banks make their money by using other people's money at one interest rate and lending it to someone else at another, higher, interest rate and pocketing the difference. But if you know *how* they do it, this will put you in the top 1% of the population and may make you think carefully about where you put your money. You might even consider stashing it under your bed.

Banks have three sources of funds that they then lend out:

- Deposits from their depositors
- Borrowing from each other
- The wider financial markets

By far the most fickle and most important of this group are the depositors like you and me. Over time the strings that tie us to banks have loosened. When the internet came along traditional bank customer loyalty all but disappeared, and deposits became a much less dependable source of funds for banks. It created a group of people called 'rate tarts' (not 'rat tart' as I first read this) who scour the internet for the most attractive rate they can find and switch accounts, usually at no cost.

But even as a 'rate tart' you should take notice of the rate you are being offered. Banks of any kind will offer a rate depending upon how desperate they are for your money or how risky the organisation is. The higher the rate the riskier the deposit-taker. So if you think the attractive rate you see advertised looks too good to be true it probably is.

As depositors we have become used to the idea that banks are, on the whole, a safe place to put all our savings. Is this true in the twenty-first century? Should I keep my money under the mattress instead? To answer those questions you have to understand how a bank works and what the future is for banking as the century progresses.

Depositors – it's a wonderful life

If you want to understand how a bank really works, become a student of the film *It's a Wonderful Life*. It is the source of all you could conceivably need to know about banking, contains all of man's frail relationship with money while simultaneously, and lavishly, illustrating how tremblingly unstable banking can be.

Take the scene just under an hour into the movie when the local evil banker, Mr Potter, causes panic to sweep through Bedford Falls. Potter has caused a 'run' on the banks. Savers descend upon the Bailey Bros Savings and Loan run by George Bailey, and they now have nearly no money left. A large crowd of depositors gathers at the counter where George speaks to them: 'You're thinking about this place all wrong: like I had all the money back in the safe ... Why, your money's in Joe's house and [pointing] that's right next to yours and the Kennedy house and Mrs Makeland's house and a hundred others.' And there you have it; we each lend to each other. The bank acts as the intermediary and it's all held together by trembling metaphysical faith.

There are wide regional variations of how much of total lending comes from lending out customers' deposits; in the US it's about 50%, in Japan a whopping 75%, in the Emerging Markets 50–70%, whereas in Europe it's about 40%. But no matter how you structure it, banking principles all over the world are exactly the same as the Bailey Savings and Loan: depositors deposit money and bankers lend it long term, taking the difference between the deposit rate and the lending rate as their profit. Sometimes, as in the case of the Bailey Savings and Loan, the depositors own the bank but more often than not it is independent shareholders who reap the rewards of the lending process. Banks hold a fraction of the total loans in cash just in case someone wants to take some out to, say, eat, hence the term 'fractional' banking. What they keep back – their reserves – they expect never to exhaust. It's what they keep back for a rainy day, in case things go wrong.

Borrow - Loans - Debt - Reserves - Work -

The Caucus Race – borrowing from each other

Looking for an additional source of funds, banks turn to each other. It's called 'wholesale funding'. I know it seems crazy but, depending upon where you are in the world, a portion of the money used to make bank profits comes from borrowing other people's deposits at other banks. Since the financial crisis of 2008 this activity has declined significantly but it is still there in various guises.

Increasingly this occurs across borders. A foreign bank may have your money even at this moment. When the credit crunch hit in 2008 Icelandic banks had built up combined loans ten times the size of their national income, two thirds of which came from abroad. This from a country whose main exports are aluminium ore, filleted fish and the music of the pop star Björk.

For this reason alone, wholesale funding of banks resembles a snake swallowing its own tail or a giant circular race. The one fatal flaw in the wholesale funding route is this: it assumes the market is open all the time and everybody can get their money back whenever they want. In fact, as we found out when the credit crisis hit, when confidence in each other evaporates so does the wholesale money market. For a bank this is really bad news. If someone rings you up (see Mr Potter for details) to ask for their money back and you have lent it out for, say, thirty years and you can't get it back you will default on the loan. If you can't find an alternative source of funds to plug the gap you go bust.

The wider markets

The other place banks get their money from is the capital markets in the form of bonds and equity.

Bonds are long-term loans. They carry a higher interest rate than deposits. Institutions, like pension funds, need income to pay for pensioners and the higher income offered by bank bonds make them attractive to this group of investors. Banks can borrow money for, say, thirty years from pension funds and lend it for thirty years to home buyers and take the difference between the two rates. But the rate a bank pays on a bank bond is higher than either the deposit or wholesale money market route, making it much less profitable. For this reason it forms a minor part of bank funding.

The final source of funding is equity, which is controversial; if things go wrong the equity holders should be the first in line to take the loss. For this reason it has been suggested that banks should rely more on equity funding and less on short-term funding as it will make them more prudent because the risks are higher. Nonetheless, if you see a bank selling extra shares you might like to ask a few questions before buying any stock. The amount of equity a bank issues has other uses. It can be used to gauge how risky a bank looks. Dividing the equity value by how much it has lent gives a measure of how 'leveraged' a bank is. A low leverage ratio combined with high credit growth is a good leading indicator that a bank is heading for trouble.

SCAM

SCAM Bank

In banking parlance, the sources of funds are called 'liabilities' because the banks are liable to others if they want their money back. The loans they make are called 'assets' because this is where their profits come from. Since you can't lend more than you have, the assets and liabilities of a bank always balance when you add them all up in their 'balance sheet'. If they don't you've got a problem – or a chief accountant with a private jet whose engines are kept running twenty-four hours a day.

Whatever the source of funds, the idea is that you lend the money at a higher rate than you borrow at. We, as consumers, who borrow through mortgages, credit cards, car loans, etc., pay the difference between the two; this is called the margin, or 'spread', which is the banks' profits.

To see how this works, let's set up a bank called Stewart Cowley Allied Mercantile Bank (SCAM Bank for short). SCAM will use all of these sources of funding to varying degrees and we'll lend it out at various rates for a range of reasons. We can then calculate the average cost of funding and the average rate of interest received. Taking one from the other gives us our spread and profit.

Liabilities	Deposits	Wholesale	Bonds	Equity	Total
Interest Rate	1	1.5	4	10	
Percentage	50%	30%	15%	5%	100%
Cost	0.5	0.5	0.6	0.5	2.1

Assets	Mortgages	Credit Cards	Car Loans	Home Improvements	Total
Interest Rate	6	8	10	12	
Percentage	60%	20%	15%	5%	100%
Benefit	3.6	1.6	1.5	0.6	7.3

In this example, the difference between the cost and benefit is 5.2%, which is a lot when you multiply it by trillions of dollars, pounds, euros, yen or whatever currency you may choose. Being in banking is a great life. But it isn't the whole story.

Two things stack the odds in favour of banks. Firstly, most people will do pretty much anything to repay what they owe; if you as an individual default on a loan it could damage your credit rating and inhibit your getting future loans. Customers' default rates on loans (even very risky credit card debt) are astonishingly low: even in the really bad times it is only a few percentage points of the total lent. If you are charging a sufficiently high interest rate on a sufficiently large book of business you can absorb even these losses without impairing your profits. People's honesty is the banker's friend.

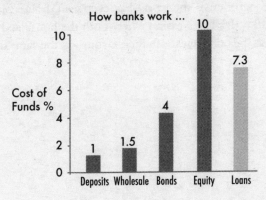

How banks work ...

Secondly, real estate prices tend to rise over time. Property, unlike, say, cars or consumer goods, have an advantage; if you get into trouble they provide you with something to sell which may be worth more than its starting value. For example, let's imagine you get a 100% mortgage on your dream home. If house prices rise at 5% a year for five years then the loan you took out would be only 78% of the value of the house. As a bank your only thought would be 'If the borrower stops paying could I sell the house and get my money back even after all the other legal fees?' Even with the modest 5% assumption the answer is a resounding 'Yes'.

And don't forget this is with a 100% mortgage; make the borrower put down 20% up front and after five years the ratio of the initial loan to the value of the property drops to 63%. In other words, as a bank, the cushion you have against making a loss is simply enormous. Knowing this you begin to appreciate why it is in just about everybody's interests, in a functioning capitalist economy, to keep house prices rising at a more or less steady pace; banks win and homeowners win.

These numbers aren't fanciful. In the US, on rolling five-year periods, house prices rose by about 5% for thirty years while in the UK it was just under 9% with barely a pause for breath. Even in Europe between 2005 and 2015, during the worst property crisis the world has ever seen, house prices rose by 19%. It's like a casino where both the house and the punter has the odds stacked in their favour – at the same time.

Man vs Banks

My daughter, who knows a thing or two about the human body, once told me, 'Breakfast doesn't count.' Her point was you could chug down a cup of goose fat for breakfast with no consequences because you are going to burn it off as you go about your day, and it isn't the thing that is going to make your waistline expand. In many ways banks are like breakfast: if you take your risks (calories) early they don't count. As a bank, all you have to do is eat as much risk as you can early on and house price appreciation and the passage of time will do all the heavy lifting for you. That plus the honesty of ordinary people.

So, having come through the worst banking crisis since 1929, thinking about whether we should trust banks in the future we only have two questions:

1. Will house and property prices keep rising?
2. How much bigger can banks get?

History tells us that the answer to the first question is that there will be lumps and bumps along the way, but continued population growth maybe until 2050 will keep property prices rising. There will be regional differences but demand for property is still set to outstrip supply.

400										
300										
200										
100										

UK   France   Netherlands   Spain   Austria   Sweden   Germany   Belgium   Italy   Japan   Poland   US

What this does to the banking system is much scarier. To give you an idea as to how big the banking system is around the world you can compare the total banking assets to the gross domestic product (GDP) of a country. In a 2013 study the Bank of England published the graphic shown above. Astonishingly, the UK, for historical reasons and because lots of foreign banks have chosen to cluster there, has a banking system four and a half times the size of its GDP. In 1975 it was just 100% of GDP.

Other countries fare little better. Much of Europe is embroiled in a banking expansion of a similar magnitude. Only the United States has a system which is a fraction of national income. However, this shouldn't give the US cause for (false) comfort: the GDP of the US is some $14 trillion while the UK is some $7 trillion.

Being big isn't, per se, a bad thing but, without strict regulations, a bloated banking system can develop, one that needs national government guarantees standing behind it. Paradoxically, creating implicit or explicit government guarantees for banks has the knock-on effect of creating the idea of 'Too Big to Fail', which, without constraints, allows banks to take excessive risks which can, in itself, give rise to a new crisis. This is one of the circular arguments that recurs in finance.

Interestingly, the same Bank of England study extrapolated the growth of the global banking sector until

2050 and found, even with modest assumptions, the UK banking system might roughly double from its current size to 950% of GDP while the median nation within the G20 club of wealthy countries would see their banking system rise to some 600% of GDP. In money terms UK banking assets would rise from £5 trillion to £60 trillion. No government could help a system out of a gargantuan-sized hole if it got into trouble: 'Too Big to Fail' would become 'Too Big to Bail'.

So, in the twenty-first century should you put your money in a bank or under the mattress? What is certain is that, as globalisation continues and incomes around the world converge towards a higher average, the banking system will continue to expand in the manner modelled by the Bank of England. Without regulation and constraint banks will become bigger and beyond the reach of government support, and it will be up to us to do our homework better than in the past before entrusting our life's savings to one institution. That tin box under the bed may come in handy after all.

6

The Markets

Should I give up my day job and play the markets for a living?

The Bloomberg system began life on Wall Street in the 1980s. In its infancy it had a tiny bespoke keyboard you had to thump just to get a response. The screen was the size of a portable television and was displayed in black and orange. Its glass screen was specially reinforced to allow angry traders to bounce the brick-like keyboard off it in times of minor irritation. It made a rather pleasing 'dink' sound when they did this.

Today, Bloomberg has blossomed into a worldwide and sophisticated network with its own television news channel and vastly sophisticated analytics. Learning to use Bloomberg is a lifetime's work. But there is hope for the amateur investor. You can now get access to real-time prices and information for trivial amounts of money.

This is a truly staggering development. Tie this to a trading account through an internet-based broker and your access to financial markets and your ability to buy and sell things

has never been greater and never been easier. Smartphone and laptop apps, real-time prices, trading account profit and losses as they happen and consolidated tax statements delivered only days after the tax year ends have made the prospect of playing the markets for a living a beguiling and very real prospect for the many. More to the point, it won't cost you the $1,000 a month for a Bloomberg terminal.

If you wanted to throw in your day job and sit there mesmerised by the numbers blinking in front of you all day, there has never been a better time to do it. With all the new twenty-first-century graphical and analytical firepower at your fingertips, shouldn't it be possible to beat the market and make a living at it at the same time?

Why you shouldn't walk home from a bar – you may never be seen again

There has always been a deep psychological desire for consistency in the world of money – after all, the holy grail of investment management is predictability. The God of

Compound Interest is a benign one if you are on the right side of it: interest consistently piled upon interest piled upon interest is, with enough time, very powerful mathematics. Time is somewhat cheap but consistency of returns, especially at the higher levels, is a pretty rare commodity.

This hasn't stopped us from trying to impose a kind of order on things in an attempt to manufacture consistency mainly through looking for patterns in price history charts of markets over the very long and short term in search of the best time to buy and sell. This is called 'technical analysis' and is practised by 'chartists', which, if you listen to some of its very committed high priests, sounds much more like a cult than an objective discipline. It even has its own mystical language and sounds something like this:

> *Chinese shares have stabilised near the lower end of a four-year trading range. Holding near 10,000 maintains the short-term double bottom pattern off the 2012–2013 lows at 9,100–8,800 and supports the case for a move back to 11,200 with resistance near 12,000. The 8,000 area provides additional support as a 50% retracement of the Fibonacci post-2007 high. The Hang Seng has underperformed relative to Asian Index but is testing big support at the relative downtrend line from late 2010 and early 2014 relative low. This is a potential positive.*

Leaving aside the problems of possessing a double bottom, in its essence technical analysis is an attempt to predict the future by coming to conclusions from lines drawn around trend lines (a chart of price movements). There is an implicit assumption behind this idea that patterns have meaning, or, more to the point, useful information inside them to guide your trading actions; when to buy and sell.

Take, for instance, the following charts of financial markets. If you stare at them long enough you will start to see patterns – lines of apparent 'support' which the price line bounces up from and which you might like to think of as a 'buy' signal. Or lines of 'resistance' the price consistently hits, like a ceiling, you might like to think of as a 'sell' signal. You might even get to see a super trend within these shorter-term patterns – despite the daily movements there is a generalised rising or falling tendency which might bring you to the conclusion that the thing creating the graph was something to own or avoid over the long term.

Do You See What I See?

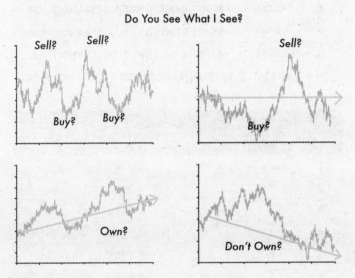

Sadly, these graphs are a trick. Each of the graphs were made using an equation using a random number generator in a spreadsheet, a right index finger and the 'Recalc' button. And for those of you who would like to have a go at reproducing these graphs (not these exact ones, obviously, because they are random and cannot ever be repeated) here it is:

Underlying Equations		
	A	B
1	Date	Value
2	1	1
3	=A2+1	=B2+IF((RAND())>0.5,1,-1)*RAND()/100
4	=A3+1	=B3+IF((RAND())>0.5,1,-1)*RAND()/100
5	=A4+1	=B4+IF((RAND())>0.5,1,-1)*RAND()/100
6	=A5+1	=B5+IF((RAND())>0.5,1,-1)*RAND()/100
7	=A6+1	=B6+IF((RAND())>0.5,1,-1)*RAND()/100
8	=A7+1	=B7+IF((RAND())>0.5,1,-1)*RAND()/100
9	=A8+1	=B8+IF((RAND())>0.5,1,-1)*RAND()/100
10	=A9+1	=B9+IF((RAND())>0.5,1,-1)*RAND()/100
11	=A10+1	=B10+IF((RAND())>0.5,1,-1)*RAND()/100

Output		
	A	B
1	Date	Value
2	1	1.000
3	2	0.991
4	3	0.993
5	4	0.986
6	5	0.993
7	6	0.992
8	7	1.001
9	8	1.008
10	9	1.011
11	10	1.009

What the equation in column B is saying is 'Whatever the number was before, randomly add or subtract a random number from it'. In other words, if there is a pattern there it's because you want to see it rather than it having any real meaning.

This randomness is why market prices have been likened to a drunken man staggering around in a field late at night. If you want to find him the next day, set off from where he started and head in a straight line in any direction you want; you have an equal probability of finding him. In other words, you just can't tell where he is going to be from the starting point. This is why prices are said to experience 'random walk' and is somewhat unhelpful if we want to give up our day job and take up trading for a living: we might just be about to get involved with a system that is inherently unpredictable. So what does make markets move?

Just another manic Monday?

The closest thing ever approaching an explanation of why markets move is called 'the efficient market hypothesis' (EMH). The EMH says all information about anything is 'in the price' and only new information or a shock makes the price move. In other words, whatever the price is today is entirely *independent* of what the price was yesterday and it is only new information driving prices.

The EMH is a very comforting idea but it has its critics. For instance, in theory any excessive price movements not supported by new information should be eradicated over time – if returns are excessively high for no reason they should be followed by negative returns: eventually everything returns

$ = New Information

Mean Average

Somewhere

Start

back to the middle or 'mean reverts'. However, there has been a tendency for stock markets since the 1960s (for instance) to display 'mean aversion' – higher returns are followed by higher returns or a general drift higher, for instance.

In some cases this process can get out of hand, leading to manic, self-feeding behaviour which eventually concludes in a crash. It's relatively easy to spot when this process is taking place. Here are just three examples from the recent past: the NASDAQ stock market index in the US between 1992 and 2002, the Brazilian stock market between 2000 and 2008 and the Nikkei-Dow stock market index in Japan between 1981 and 1990. The change in value is shown in terms of how many times they rose compared to their starting value when the mania kicked off. For instance, the NASDAQ rose eight times, or 800%, during its ascent.

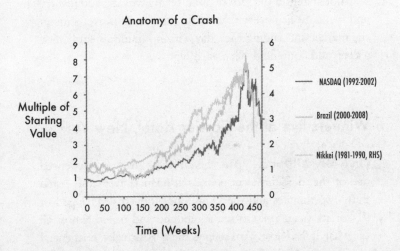

Anatomy of a Crash

Although these examples happened at different times, these so-called 'asset bubbles' display very similar characteristics, which look like this:

- A new socio-economic paradigm appears with no visible or possible ending.
- All opposition to the new paradigm is countered with supporting documentation convincing investors of consistent, riskless returns.
- The shape of the ensuing price mania has an accelerating trend to it which ends after returns are multiples of the starting point eight to ten years previously.
- The trend ends very suddenly and unpredictably and the market loses about half of what was made in a fraction of the time it took to get there.

It's easy, even if you can see it happening, to be swept up in a market mania, and even if you enter into it knowingly, getting out before the bubble goes 'pop' is a difficult exercise. So why not abandon the idea of long-term investing and just try and make money every day, trading the small movements in the market and ending each day with no holdings, and enjoy a deep and contented sleep each night?

Winners live at the Carrier Hotel, New York

On 6 May 2010 at 2.45 p.m. the US stock market experienced one of the most turbulent periods in financial history. It lasted thirty-two minutes and the Dow Jones Industrial Average lost 9% of its value, only to see it rebound and regain almost all of what it had lost. Amazingly, there is actually no general agreement as to what the exact mechanism was that caused the Flash Crash of 2.45 p.m. What is agreed is that high-frequency trading had something to do with it.

Be wary of asset bubbles ...

they are prone to bursting

High-frequency trading, or HFT as it is known, has become more and more prevalent in the markets. The use of computers and the programs (called algorithms) has now reached epidemic levels in the financial system. It accounts for some 70% of all trading on stock markets each day without any adult supervision. What could possibly go wrong, you might ask?

For day traders, the people who attempt to trade the micromarkets' movements within a day, 'you snooze – you lose' has never been more real or what we define as 'snoozing' so brief. To increase the speed of trading by just eight microseconds, some high-frequency traders moved closer and closer to the Carrier Hotel in mid-town Manhattan, New York. To put this into perspective, it takes you about 5,000 microseconds to click the mouse on your computer. The Carrier Hotel is the place where the main feed for the internet emerges for the entire city of New York. Moving closer to it gives you a fractional advantage over your competitors.

What is also deeply unnerving about HFT algorithms is that now other predatory algorithms search them out, work out their patterns and start trading against them. In other words there is a network of computers talking to each other and trading hundreds of thousands of times a second without any human intervention. What this does is introduce a degree of randomness *within a day*, which means even professional institutions, never mind individual investors, have little chance of competing against the high-frequency traders. Being a day trader and consistantly beating the market has never been harder and may even be impossible.

Getting out before the bubble goes

* pop *

is a difficult exercise...

Man vs The Markets

Markets always have been and always will be unpredictable –
the random walk of the fund manager on the way home from
the wine bar is manifest of what they do in office hours, it
seems. Despite the best efforts of technical analysts or those
who believe in company fundamentals, or investors using
economics as their yardstick for their investment decisions,
there doesn't appear to be a single theory to describe why
in the short, or even the long, term, financial markets do
what they do. In this age of ubiquitous visuals, we should
be careful not to be seduced by flashy graphics that give the
illusion of analysis when it is our brains that are projecting a
desired result onto the information.

Layer on top the influence of high-frequency trading,
and you have a heady cocktail best drunk only in single shots
– our tipsy fund manager just became a whole lot more
intoxicated, you might say. This is somewhat unnerving if
you were contemplating giving up your day job to trade the
markets or have cash to spare and want to put it to work today.

The good news is we are now better at spotting manias
when we see them. If you do have access to today's investment
technology you are now in a better position than ever before
to avoid some of the obvious mistakes and not get drawn
into the manias you don't choose to be involved in. It might

even give you a fighting chance of beating the market over the very long term and help secure your financial future. But, tempting though it may be, don't give up your day job just yet.

7

Virtual Money

Should I get paid in bitcoin?

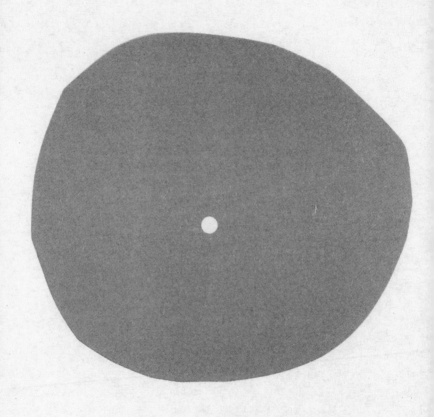

Ever since the Yap islanders of the Pacific Ocean first asked, 'Have you got change for one of these?', pointing at a twelve-foot-diameter stone with a hole in the middle, we have been searching for a more convenient way of exchanging value between us without the need for a crane. We have tried all kinds of things:

- Soap
- Cocoa
- Beans
- Elephants
- Parts of elephants
- Livestock
- Sea snail shells
- Gold

The list is pretty much endless and bewilderingly diverse but all the above have one thing in common – they had or have a rarity or some other kind of value projected onto them that caused us to accumulate them as the global economy expanded. But eventually, as wealth increased, all of them became too bulky or inconvenient to move around in large quantities. In the case of livestock, it had the habit of either dying or running away. There had to be a better way to do this.

Then, one day, we hit upon the idea of keeping a lot of gold under lock and key and writing notes saying, 'I promise to pay the bearer on demand the equivalent of …' against it. From then on we could circulate the notes and coins and leave the gold where it was. The amount of paper money in society was equal to the amount of gold locked away in the vaults. You couldn't have more money than gold and all you had to do was find ingenious ways of stopping people from forging the bank notes, which turns out to be the second oldest profession in the world.

This is how we alighted upon paper money (which is actually made of linen). Although the Chinese had used paper money in the ninth century AD its tendency to blow away in the wind kept it in abeyance until France began using it in earnest in the eighteenth century. Since then our love affair with paper money has been both touching and stormy.

All went well for a long time and then, in the twentieth century, we abandoned the idea that money had to be backed by gold, or some other commodity, and instead said, 'Trust me ... I'm a country. Look at all the land with things on it I have. Surely you'll accept this piece of paper?!'

This approach has had varying degrees of success and more notable failures. Because if you start producing something nobody wants any more the value (price) of it goes down. If you start producing even more of it to compensate for the previous decline in value then the downward spiral speeds up. For a nation this can be catastrophic – the inflation this creates can reach epidemic proportions. In 2008, Zimbabwe experienced inflation of 6.5 sextillion per cent just by printing valueless money.

Consistently printing money backed by nothing but metaphysical faith, has made a lot of people suspicious of it and in the process, created a gap in the system. So, today, do we have a way of storing value which isn't in the control of capricious governments? Or subject to sudden economic shocks? And can be used for transactions all over the world without transaction costs? Enter, stage right, "virtual currencies". On the face of it, they sound so good you would have to wonder why we are bothering with national currencies at all and makes you wonder why we aren't demanding our employers pay us in them.

What is a bitcoin?

The virtual currency you have probably heard of is Bitcoin. It works like this: imagine a great big warehouse with rows and rows of shelves. On these shelves there are lots of identical

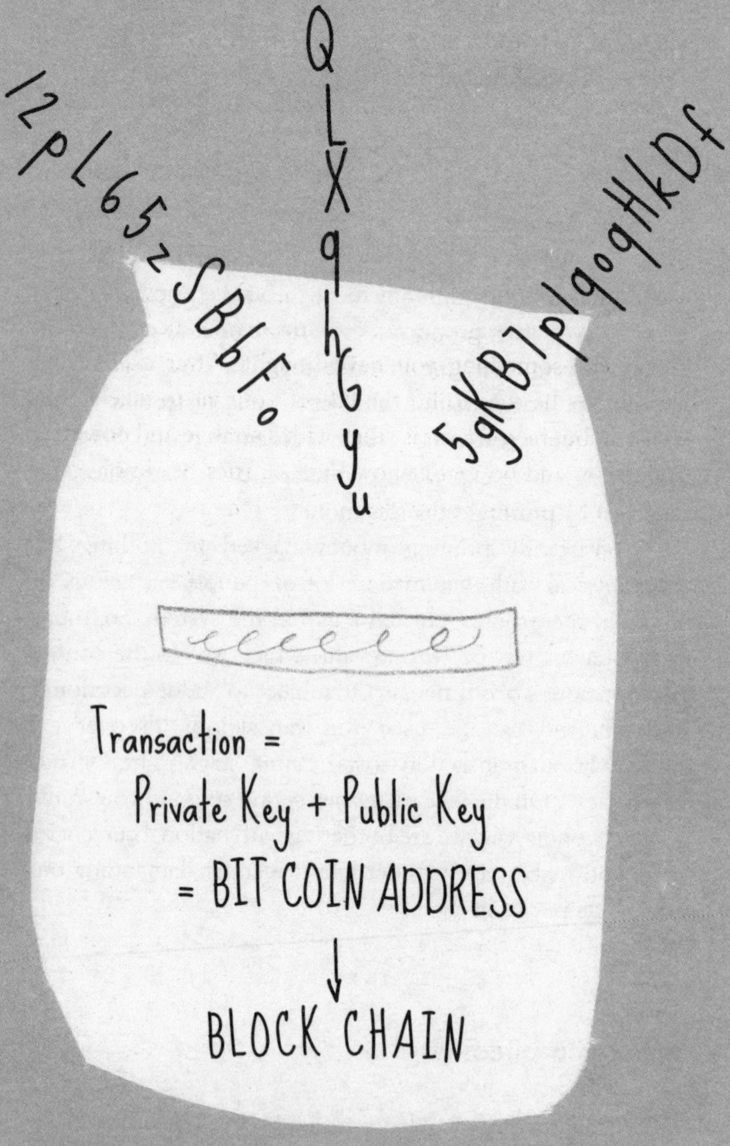

12pL65zSBbFo

QLXqhGyu

5gKB7plqoqHkDf

Transaction =
Private Key + Public Key
= BIT COIN ADDRESS
↓
BLOCK CHAIN

glass jars with what looks like a random looking series of letters and numbers on them:

12pL6SzSBbFoQLXqhGyu5gkB7p1qoqHkDf

Inside the jars are coins. But there is a twist – the jar is fiercely loyal to you and you alone.

You have arranged to meet somebody at the warehouse to pay for something you have bought. After exchanging pleasantries he tries to lift the lid off your jar to take a coin out of it, but he can't – it is stuck with a strange and powerful magnetism and no matter how hard he tries he simply can't budge it. However, you whisper something to your jar, and lightly lift the lid off. You take out a coin and hand it to him and he whispers something to his jar, lifts the lid off and pops the money in. You then walk over to a guy wearing a miner's helmet who is poring over a large book. In this book you register the fact that you have transferred one coin from you to your companion. The miner writes it down and for his troubles a bitcoin drops out of thin air, which he furtively pockets. Everyone departs, slightly confused but nonetheless happy.

This virtual glass jar-filled world is how bitcoin would work if it was a physical entity. The letters and numbers on the side of the jar is what is known as a bitcoin personal address. The 'secret word' you whisper to open your jar is called the 'private key' and allows you to *spend* bitcoins. The personal address and your private key are mathematically related to each other but nobody will ever be able to work out how. But be warned - lose your private key and you have lost access to spending your bitcoins.

To *receive* bitcoins, you need a 'public key'. Your public key is mathematically related in a unique way to your private key. Your public key combined with your address is what allows people to send you bitcoins. The intertwining of your public key, private key and personal address is what keeps the system secure.

You can have more than one bitcoin address (just as you can have more than one email address) but each one will have its own private and public key. The keys are kept on your computer in what's known as a bitcoin wallet. Lose the wallet and you lose all access to your jars. If someone steals your wallet they can empty your jars.

The slightly misleading thing about the jar/meeting place analogy is that, in the world of virtual currencies, there is no physical place where you can go, or electronic repository of bitcoins. In reality there is merely a big book or ledger showing all the transactions there have ever been which adds up to all the bitcoins in existence and who owns what at each bitcoin address. The ledger is called 'the block chain' and a group of people called 'miners' really do spend their days verifying bitcoin transactions for which they are paid in newly created bitcoins.

The block chain isn't in one place – a network of computers have their own copy of it. When people perform a bitcoin transaction one of these computers picks them up in a block and broadcasts it to the other computers. It is then that the block is tacked on (or chained) to the existing ledger. Only new blocks can be added – the old ones can't be changed. What you end up with is a running total of who owns what with an incontrovertible history.

Building your wallet bit by bit

Any currency needs to be exchangeable – be it for goods, services or hard cash – to be of use and therefore of true value. Perhaps the biggest difference between virtual currency and money as we know it is that you can't make a bitcoin. Well, ordinary people can't (the freakish miners get the new ones). You can only get bitcoins by engaging in a bitcoin transaction and having them credited to your address. Right now there are three ways to use your coins:

1. Direct trades: Websites allowing you to sell virtual currencies for cash include Coinbase and LocalBitcoins in the US, and BitBargain UK and Bittylicious in the UK.

2. Exchange trades: Exchanges act as a middleman and hold everyone's funds in hard currencies like US dollars, the euro etc. If you want to transact you place an order (to buy or sell) along with the amount, stating the type of virtual currency and the price you want. As soon as someone places a matching order, the exchange completes the transaction and the proceeds are then credited to your account.

3. Peer-to-peer trading marketplaces: The marketplace acts as an intermediary between various groups. The first group consists of individuals who want to be able to use virtual currencies to buy goods from sites not currently accepting digital currencies. The second comprises others who would like to buy a virtual currency with credit or debit cards. The marketplace brings together individuals with matching requirements to effectively sell bitcoin to one and provide goods for the other.

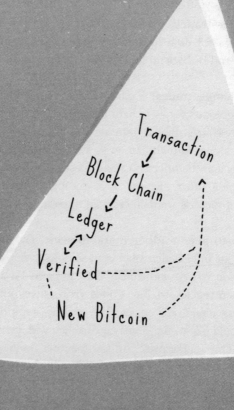

Transaction
Block Chain
Ledger
Verified
New Bitcoin

Apart from these three places to obtain and trade bitcoins there is perhaps the strangest way to make your virtual wallet bulge: 'mining'. We have already touched on miners, but they do warrant a more detailed mention. Miners play a competitive game all day, every day. Every ten minutes Bitcoin sets a puzzle to find a random number within a range based on the last set of transactions in the block chain. At any one time there are hundreds of thousands of computers whirring away trying to solve the puzzle first. If you get it right you win twenty-five bitcoins which are then credited to your address and you get the right to add the new transactions to the block chain.

Right now there are 150 bitcoins being created every hour, which is 3,600 a day or 1,314,000 a year. But Bitcoin have said they will reduce this by half every year going forwards and have placed an upper limit of about 21,000,000 bitcoins to be created by the year 2140. In other words there is a finite supply of bitcoins.

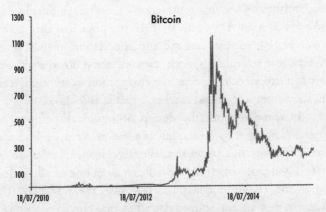

Mining has another function besides acting as a way of creating coins. It is used for securing the block chain. Each successful miner submits the solution to the puzzle they answered. Others can then verify their solution (which is 'easy' once it's known) and this becomes 'proof-of-work'. The transactions are then added to the block chain in the knowledge they are unique (i.e. no conflicting transactions are added simultaneously) and the ledger adds up again. In this sense, virtual mining is the same as digging up gold. The digger shows his gold, it's verified for authenticity and added to the gold bank – except it's better, as it's all done from the comfort of one's computer.

Bitcoin, in common with other virtual currencies, has properties that ordinary currencies simply don't possess. Not least of these oddities is the problem of supply and demand. The supply angle has been settled for bitcoin at least by the pledge that, like commodities such as gold or silver, there is going to be a finite amount of bitcoins created.

However, as with any commodity, sudden excesses in demand can do strange things to a virtual currency. For instance, when Satoshi Nakamoto launched the currency and performed the first transaction in 2009, each bitcoin was worth just a few US cents. In 2013 the price had shot up to over $1,140 because demand and speculation, mainly from China, was so high. It quickly came crashing down again but bitcoin experienced a price movement more commonly seen in the commodity markets when a mania takes hold.

In some respects the design of bitcoin anticipates an increase in value over time but at a less manic pace. You can trade fractions of a bitcoin and they have names: a millibitcoin (10^{-3}), a microbitcoin (10^{-6}) and the smallest one of all, named after the inventor, Satoshi Nakamoto, the satoshi (10^{-8}). Clearly, they are expecting a day when one bitcoin is going to be worth a lot of money.

It's difficult to have a discussion about virtual currencies without raising the spectre of criminal behaviour. The public addresses certainly lend virtual currencies a level of anonymity but because all transactions are visible through the block chain you can be watched and eventually traced. For this reason virtual currencies are referred to as being pseudonymous. Still, it doesn't stop people from trying it on. In a recent cyber-attack on the UK telecommunications company TalkTalk in which thousands of customers' credit card and bank details were stolen, the $122,000 (£80,000) ransom demand was made in, yes, you guessed it, bitcoin. It took just forty-eight hours to find the Belfast schoolboy responsible for the attack.

Man vs Virtual Money

So in the future should we get paid in bitcoin rather than your national currency? At first glance bitcoin, or any other so-called virtual currency, looks like and seems to function as a currency. But the more time you spend (and the more coins you spend), the more it starts to look like something quite different. It begins to look like a commodity.

To see this, let's draw up a table of characteristics. If you compare bitcoin to a currency and commodity and then start ticking off the occasions when bitcoin is the same as a commodity (the fifth column in the table), you begin to see, more often than not, that it looks like a commodity rather than a currency.

	Bitcoin	Currency	Commodity	Bitcoin similar to a Commodity?
Can you physically hold it?	✗	✓	✓	✗
Is it controlled by a Central Bank?	✗	✓	✗	✓
Can you dig it up?	✓	✗	✓	✓
Does it pay interest?	✗	✓	✗	✓
Can it get lost?	✓	✓	✓	✓
Is it in finite supply?	✓	✗	✓	✓
Is it backed by a country?	✗	✓	✗	✓
Can it be exchanged for goods and services	✓	✓	✗	✗
It is tradeable on an exchange?	✓	✗	✓	✓
Is its value volatile?	✓	✓	✓	✓

This is a mesmerising possibility and lies behind some of the strong criticisms of virtual currencies. Journalists, economists and some central bankers have wondered out loud whether the whole bitcoin experiment isn't a massive fraud perpetrated in public. This has led to numerous obituaries being written for bitcoin and also large questions being raised about its real value. Some people have suggested its true value is zero while others suggest it could one day reach a value of $40,000. In reality the issues surrounding bitcoin's true nature and valuation remains much more uncertain than the promoters of bitcoin would have us believe. Even so, venture capitalists pumped $46 billion into companies associated with bitcoin last year. In 2012, they invested just £2 billion.

The interesting thing for twenty-first-century money is, if bitcoin and other virtual currencies actually take off and become mainstream in our world, we will have come full circle with our relationship with money: instead of exchanging sophisticated pieces of paper we will be back to where the people of the Pacific Yap Islands and their enormous mined stones were, except this time they will be stored electronically and invisibly.

Can you have
a virtual
commodity?

8

Government finances

How can a country go bust?

The English king, Richard the Lionheart wasn't who many people think he was. First of all he was French and secondly he was something of a calamitous adventurer with a gift for PR. Richard's triumphant return to England in about 1194 masks the fact that the country had just paid the Holy Roman Emperor, Henry VI, £100,000 ransom for his release following a botched return from a crusade. Given that the taxes extracted from his realm were about £30,000 a year at the time it was a heavy price to pay. The statue of him outside the Houses of Parliament in London stands as much for 'You see this – we won't be doing this again' as it does for his military prowess.

When Richard suddenly, and shockingly, died in the spring of 1199 from a speculative crossbow bolt fired by a man using a frying pan as a shield, he had at least succeeded in one respect: he had embedded in the minds of the people the idea that when the Exchequer is empty the people will be asked to fill it. His predecessors had been, frankly, amateurish in this regard. Richard's historical precedent established an important idea: governments have no money. All they have is the taxes they receive supplemented by the money they can borrow.

Having the ability to borrow money as a country has, at times, been too tempting for some. It would have been difficult to avoid the coverage of the near-collapse of Greek society in 2015. Gradually the extent of their borrowing was revealed to be thirty billion euros (over 200% of their annual income) with little or no chance of their ever paying the money back. Greece is not an isolated case: Argentina, Mexico, Nigeria, Russia, Vietnam, to name but a few, have all reneged on their debts since the 1980s. But how does it happen and will the twenty-first century be the century when failing to pay back your debts becomes the norm?

Monte Carlo or bust?

Just like people, governments borrow money and on a regular basis. The interest rate governments pay varies over time with the general level of interest rates and how good their credit is perceived to be. But if a country builds up a lot of debt over time it can be at the whim of the market and maybe events outside its control. Under the right circumstances, no matter who or what you are, if the interest you have to pay begins to exceed your ability to pay, you can go bust (or 'default' as they say).

To show you how this can happen let's invent a country called Stewartland. If a country were a household then you would probably judge its ability to pay by how much it earned (its gross GDP). Let's start off the GDP of Stewartland at 100 and debts of a modest 80, or 80% of GDP. The average interest rate Stewartland is paying is a very reasonable 2.5%. So in year one interest rate payments alone will be $80 \times 0.025 = 2$ units.

Also Stewartland is running an annual overdraft, or budget deficit, of an unspectacular 3% of GDP a year, meaning it has to raise new debt of 3 units in year one. There will be interest to pay on the first year's deficit of 0.1 at the current interest rate. So the total interest is 2.1 units in the first year or 2.1% plus the 3% from the deficit of GDP which is a total of 5.1 units (see opposite, far right column).

Now add the 5.1 units onto your outstanding debt in the first year so it is now 85.1 in year two. I've been generous and allowed some economic growth for a while – GDP rises in the second column. As you would expect, borrowing costs start to rise as the economic cycle progresses but it's OK – everything is still manageable. By year number four the debt to GDP ratio is $95.6/106 = 90.2\%$ but the budget deficit is

Year	GDP	Debt	Average Interest Rate	Interest Rate Payments	Deficit	New Debt	Interest on New Debt	Total Increase
1	100	80.0	2.5%	2.0	3.0%	3.0	0.1	5.1
2	103	85.1	3.0%	2.6	2.5%	2.6	0.1	5.2
3	105	90.3	3.5%	3.2	2.0%	2.1	0.1	5.3
4	106	95.6	4.0%	3.8	1.5%	1.6	0.1	5.5
5	107	101.1	4.5%	4.5	2.0%	2.1	0.1	6.8
6	107	107.9	5.0%	5.4	3.0%	3.2	0.2	8.8
7	105	116.7	5.5%	6.4	4.0%	4.2	0.2	10.8
8	101	127.5	6.0%	7.7	5.0%	5.0	0.3	13.0
9	96	140.5	6.5%	9.1	6.0%	5.7	0.4	15.3
10	90	155.7	7.0%	10.9	7.0%	6.3	0.4	17.6

GDP x AIR = £ DEBT

80 x 2.5 = 2

+

0.1 + 2.1 = 2.1 + 3% of GDP

= 5.1 units

falling as the economy expands due to the taxes coming in. All is still good.

But then in year seven the economy turns downwards. The debt to GDP ratio has increased from 80% to 116.7/105, or 111%, because of accumulated debts and interest payments. At the same time a new government is elected which promises to spend its way out of the economic downturn by slashing taxes and increasing government expenditure. Investors start to wonder whether they will be able to pay their debts and begin to lose confidence, pushing Stewartland's borrowing costs up. Now the average interest rate being paid by Stewartland is 5.5%, which is more than double the 2.5% starting point in year one. At the same time the deficit expands because politicians are unable to cut public expenditure or raise taxes.

The spiralling debt to GDP ratio and mounting interest bill cause the ratings agencies to cut Stewartland's credit rating. Investors now demand an even higher interest rate to compensate them for the risk of default. In year eight, with the economy now shrinking, the debt to GDP ratio has risen to 126%. With the whiff of default in the air, Stewartland is at the mercy of day-to-day news flow. News teams gather outside the Central Bank. Each new attempt to raise more debt is watched as if it is a game show. Stewartland is now living hand to mouth. Investors drain money from the banking system via internet transfers. Capital flight is occurring.

The twin problems of a rising budget deficit, compounding every year, and rising interest costs because of the discounting effect of prices falling and yields rising, kick in. After ten years over 12% of each year's GDP is being paid out as interest payments. The debt to GDP ratio is now 173%. Only three years after the beginning of the crisis this country is now on the way to going bust …

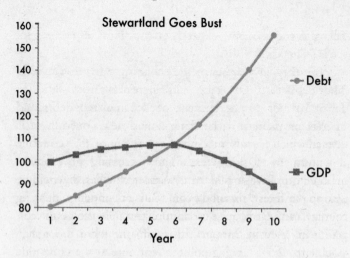

Stewartland Goes Bust

Glorious isolation?

If this sounds familiar it's because it's pretty much what Greece and countless other countries have been through in the past, in their own variations. And a lot of it is just maths. But if you think the starting point is fanciful, take a look at this.

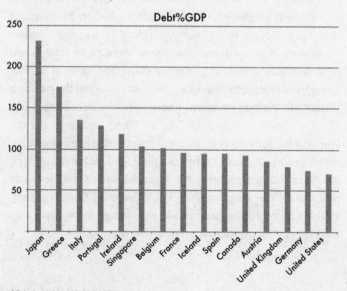

Debt%GDP

This is a graph of the government debt to GDP ratios of some of the most affluent nations in the world. A lot of these governments have debts close to the starting point of our model. What's more, about half of them habitually run up deficits greater than Stewartland's making you wonder where 'safe' is any more if you want a higher return on your cash than is being offered on deposit at your bank.

Another way to look at national finances is the concept of the 'primary surplus'. Put simply, this asks whether, ignoring interest payments on your outstanding debt, a country can afford its expenditure through the taxes it is taking in. Viewed through this prism the picture is much less alarming – almost all the countries in the world, including the most scarily indebted like Japan, Greece and Italy, run a primary surplus. Their problem is their interest payments. If, for whatever reason, their cost of borrowing begins to increase that is when the problems start. Our old friend compound interest takes over and events take a different course.

Failing in your ability to pay or meet your interest payments, there are two things you can do:

- Ask for forgiveness from your creditors and ask them to cancel what you owe.
- Devalue your currency to such a point that the debt is worthless.

The first route is fraught with difficulty and danger, not the least of which is our interconnectedness. You have to make sure other financial institutions around the world which may have lent you money aren't taken down with you. In the short term it offers a fix to the situation – debt cancellation reduces both the size of and the interest you have to pay. But the downside is that one day you will want to borrow money again. And if you have reneged on your obligations once you can do it again. The markets will demand a premium for your new riskiness in the form of a higher interest rate.

If you have your own currency you could just devalue it or let the markets do it for you. In this case the value of your debt will decline to external holders, your economy will get a positive kick because your goods and services will be cheaper on the international markets and GDP will rise considerably. The ratios by which you are measured (debt to GDP, etc.) improve markedly and it can, effectively, reset the clock for you as a nation. The cost is that national inflation will rise rapidly, the value of savings is wiped out and the nation is generally impoverished for a period of time. When this happened in Argentina in 1989 the cost of a carton of milk changed in the time it took to enter a shop, pick it off the shelf and pay for it at the counter. It is not an easy or costless route out of the debt trap.

Man vs Government Finances

On the face of it we never really abandoned John Maynard Keynes and his vision of government expenditure. Western government expenditure has risen consistently since 1900 and accelerated since the Second World War, no matter whether the right or left in politics has been in power. For many nations government expenditure as a proportion of GDP wasn't more than a few per cent at the turn of the last century. As we stand today, some 30–40% of GDP comes from government spending, leading to a chronic build-up of debt even in the so-called developed nations; as we have seen it is common for government debts to equal an entire year's income and more. If you were a householder with those kinds of debts you'd be getting a bit nervous at this point. The response has been an attempt to cut back on central government expenditure to slow the rate of debt accumulation. This is likely to be a major theme in the twenty-first century.

Nations could increase taxes or pursue a persistent campaign to close tax loopholes in order to gather the revenue national governments need to balance the books. Increasing taxes is easy but many studies show it can be counter-productive to an overall economy. Meanwhile, taking government expenditure out of society is a painful thing to do: someone, somewhere, is going to lose out and more often than not it is the people who need it the most who will bear the brunt. Many find this an unpalatable prospect and choose to vote for political parties advocating the expansion of government spending, possibly combined with devaluation.

One of the things we have learned about the aftershocks from financial crises is that after a period of time countries experience a decisive political swing to either the left or the right. Either way, candidates who promise increasing expenditure in the face of already stretched finances might be appealing to the electorate in the short term but will be dicing with the consequences of compound interest further down the line.

So it may come down to the political and democratic choices that we make dictating whether a major debtor nation goes bust in the twenty-first century. The choices we make, as citizens, will guide the direction of travel but, ultimately, compound interest will dictate the timing.

9

Millions

Who wants to be
a millionaire?

Becoming a 'millionaire' has a timeless attraction: mankind's aspirations to possess the sense of limitless possibility combined with the intellectual and emotional freedom that comes with it is, to many, almost irresistible. To achieve millionaire status requires you to boost your wealth beyond everyday notions of mere survival, or even being dependent upon fickle things such as having a job, and into an altogether new place.

In October 2009 the American chat show host David Letterman made an unusual announcement live on television. He was being blackmailed. When he informed the audience the ransom was two million dollars, among the laughter there was a sharp intake of breath followed by an astonished 'Whooooa!!!', to which Letterman gave a sideways glance and retorted with a wry smile on his face, '*Is that the foreigners?*' Clearly, in the twenty-first century two million US dollars isn't what it used to be – our relationship with this iconic quantum of money has changed.

Also, being a 'millionaire' means different things to different people: one million Japanese yen is about $8,500 at today's exchange rate so to be a yen millionaire isn't saying much. If you really want to flatter yourself you could go to Hungary where you can become a forint millionaire for just $3,400. So, right from the start, you have to understand what you are judging your notions of financial independence against and then work out, given today's money, what you need to truly attain the title 'millionaire'.

Are you already a secret millionaire?

Being a millionaire isn't as straightforward as you might think. First of all, are you talking about 'wealth' or 'income'? One approach to finding out if you are a millionaire is to add up all your household's wealth and subtract its debts. So if you lived in a home worth $800,000, possessed $150,000 worth of contents, had savings of $250,000 (total $1,200,000) but a mortgage and loans of $150,000 then the difference would be $1,050,000 and you might like to think of yourself as a millionaire. Congratulations!

Or not. Other definitions of millionaires exclude things like your main home, contents and cars and are only interested in ready cash or savings you can spend, invest or even lose without it causing you too much hardship. Our household described here would only have $100,000 in this case and it would now slump back into the non-millionaire status once more. Easy come, easy go.

Millionaire: independent wealth or personal income?

You might like to think of a millionaire as someone who has an income each year of more than a million dollars. There are two ways you can get that kind of money – you can earn it or you can get it from investments in the form of interest (from deposits, stock dividends or bond interest).

Earning a million dollars a year is a pretty rarified thing and relies upon having a job which can be somewhat precarious at that level of income even if you are self-employed. What we are talking about here is how to live the lifestyle of a millionaire, in perpetuity, without really having to think about it. In other words, how do you generate an investment income from the financial markets that finances a millionaire lifestyle and how much money do you need to have saved to do that?

Some economists believe that the global economy in the twenty-first century is caught in the grip of a persistent low inflation/low interest rate world, which is good if you are a borrower but less exciting if you are a saver and even less exciting if you want to lead a millionaire's lifestyle on passively received income.

This low income world leaves most investors who have anything other than very speculative grade investments generating an income of maybe 2–4%. Higher rates of income tax in the developed world are surprisingly uniform and average out somewhere around the 40% mark. If you follow the calculation through, then, to live the life of a millionaire, defined as a post-tax income of $250,000, you will have to accumulate assets (investments) somewhere between ten and twenty-one million dollars (see below).

As if this wasn't bad enough, if we go back to the times when the word 'millionaire' really started to come into common use, around the beginning of the twentieth century, and look at the modern equivalent, the numbers become dispiritingly large.

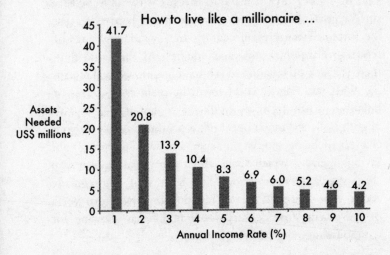

How to live like a millionaire ...

If you used the price of gold to bring the status of millionaire up to date, the equivalent amount you will need rockets to $61 million. Using another measure, the relative increase in wages, the entry price to the New Millionaire's Club rises to $162 million. But to truly enter as an elite group, the sort who swaggered around the hotels and restaurants of emerging 1900s America and built lavishly monumental estates, today you would need a bank balance groaning under the weight of $640 million. In other words, in the twenty-first century to be a millionaire you need to be on your way to being a US dollar billionaire to separate you from the herd. Faced with this daunting prospect it is little wonder a recent survey found that 28% of people with $1–5 million to their name didn't feel wealthy: a sense of limitless security only kicks in when you get above $5 million. Even this could be misplaced confidence.

If we set our sights a little lower and we had an ambition to be a millionaire through savings and investment, what kind of money do you have to invest each year to achieve such a goal? The problem is made much harder because the forces of the present century are towards low rates of return from cash, bonds and equities. At the same time, there is a lack of inflation which has compressed real returns (i.e. what you might expect from the markets in excess of inflation) down from about 3–4% to about 1–2%. This might not sound much but it has a profound effect on your chances of being, at least on paper, a millionaire during your savings lifetime, which spans about thirty-five years if you are particularly conscientious. For instance, if you regularly add to your savings in the low inflation and low return world of the twenty-first century you'll find, even allowing for compounding, the following is true:

- You have to save about $9,700 every year for thirty-five years (and increase your contribution each year by inflation) to have, on paper, $1,000,000 at the end of it.
- To have $1,000,000 in real terms (i.e. allowing for inflation) your annual contribution rises to nearly $19,400 from year one.

You have to say not many people have that kind of money to sink into the financial markets. Not many people have that kind of patience either; the essence of being a millionaire is to have it *now* rather than in thirty-five years' time. Saving your way to millionaire status isn't a viable option.

Who are the new millionaires?

If you are interested in money it goes without saying that people like Bill Gates ($79 billion) and Carlos Slim Helú ($77 billion) are interesting people occupying, as they do, first and second place on the global rich list. The magnitude of their wealth has travelled so far away from what is conceivable to the human mind, it is difficult to comprehend. At least we can be grateful for the thought the world has not, so far, produced a trillionaire but it is only a matter of time: if you started off with Bill and Slim's sort of money, it would only take you about fifty years at an annual return of 5% to become the first trillionaire. The twenty-first century *will* produce a trillionaire...

Bill Gates and his fellow rich listers have achieved the billions needed to lead the lifestyle of limitless possibility of 1900s millionaires. They are the new millionaires. To find out who the new millionaires are and how they got there you don't have to look at the top of annual wealth league tables, like the Forbes 500 Rich List, but towards the bottom. This is the place where the new entrants and the old declining dynasties can be found. So who are they and can we get some clues from them if we want to be a twenty-first-century millionaire?

To find out who the real new millionaires are you need to meticulously research the biography and business history of the bottom 100 of the Forbes 500 Rich List – where some strange happenings will pop out at you. Strikingly, today, to get into the bottom 100 of the Forbes list, you now need in excess of $3 billion.

The range of routes to wealth for this group are truly staggering – the wealthy in the twenty-first century aren't who we might think they are. They usually aren't born into

The twenty-first century will produce a trillionaire...

money, they didn't steal it and they don't even come from an intellectual elite. They are much more likely to have come from nothing, earned their wealth in their own lifetime and, in a striking number of cases, left school at an early age. Within this group there are some fascinating stories. These are just some of them:

- Haim Saban, the bass player in the minor rock band The Lions of Judah, realised management was the way to go and made $3.5 billion from it. It didn't stop him from keeping his hand in musically: he went on to pen the theme song for *Mighty Morphin Power Rangers: The Movie*.
- Isaac Perlmutter, who built a $3.8 billion fortune from Marvel comics but, despite working in publishing, has never given an interview and has only ever been accidentally photographed in public.
- Bernie Ecclestone ($3.9 billion) left school at sixteen to become a laboratory technician and somehow ended up owning the Formula One motor racing franchise.

- Fred Smith's disarmingly simple name didn't stop him from writing an alarmingly forward-looking undergraduate paper at Yale in 1962 outlining an overnight delivery service in the computer age. Legend has it that he received a 'C' grade for his efforts but in the process he did at least create FedEx.
- And, finally, who would have thought Miuccia Prada would not only be a mime artist for five years but also gain a doctorate in political science before turning her attentions to handbags and making $4.1 billion in the process.

As of 2015 you needed over $3.5 billion just to make it onto the Forbes list. As recently as the turn of the millennium you could have made it there with less than $1 billion. Membership of the New Millionaire's Club seems to be receding from us as quickly as we appear to be approaching it.

Man vs Millions

There is obviously an upper limit to the amount of money anyone should acquire in their lifetime mainly for their own good. Felix Dennis, who amassed a fortune of over a billion dollars from publishing before his death in 2014, was a classic rags to riches story and his take on wealth was refreshingly clear – you only need to accumulate a few million, after which you are wasting your life.

But if you do want to become a member of the New Millionaire's Club it's pretty clear you don't want to be a millionaire – you want to be a billionaire. Sadly, even winning the lottery isn't going to be enough to get you past the doorman: Gloria MacKenzie of Zephyrhills, Florida, pocketed 'only' $370 million for her world record Powerball win, which wouldn't get her over the line in terms of our new definition of what it is to be a millionaire. At the same time working for a company, unless you are a particularly rapacious CEO, as a salaried individual or saving your way to the New Millionaire's Club isn't viable, especially when we live in a century which has seen low wage growth combine with historically low real returns from investments.

There really is no two ways about it: if you want to be an old-style millionaire and live a financially carefree life you have to have an idea and start a business.

There is some good news from all of this. Some people believe the long-term effect of the financial crisis and the low interest rates it has created in the twenty-first century will persist for a very long time – maybe even decades. Coincidentally, there is a large amount of money available from savers needing an income. The combination of low interest rates and an excess of money creates ideal conditions for starting a business. There has never been a better time to put a good idea into action and in the decades to come it's going to be your best route to becoming a millionaire.

10

Quantitative easing

Are you a member of Generation QE?

Once we used only interest rates and government spending (with some tinkering with taxation on the side) to get us out of economic slumps. But then someone remembered quantitative easing (QE). Although QE had been used in Japan for decades, it wasn't something anyone in the west had had to resort to in a generation or more.

Quantitative easing is the mechanism whereby central banks buy financial assets in order to keep the financial system afloat. They do this by pressing a button to say, 'This money now exists', in the process 'manufacturing' the money out of thin air. It's one of the perks of being a central bank. The central banks now go out into the financial markets and buy financial assets (primarily bonds but some stocks also) for their own account, and hand out money to the sellers in the process. The money now in society is assumed to be employed doing some good, such as being spent on consumption and investment in new businesses, buoying the economy. But the main effect is to increase the value of bonds, stocks and (by association) real estate – the things that comprise most people's wealth.

The amount of money involved today in the global QE programme is truly, mind-bogglingly, large. The US has bought over \$4.5 trillion of assets from the markets. If you printed it out in dollar bills and spread it out over Manhattan you would be literally wading through them knee-deep. The Bank of England bought nearly £400 billion of securities and now owns some 40% of its own government bond market. Japan, which has been at this longer, owns ¥55 trillion of assets, which is nearly all of its own government bond market. In the process the Japanese government bond market has all but ceased to function as a market. Lately, the European Central Bank has adopted a 'whatever it takes' programme but it is unlikely to pause before it has accumulated €1.1 trillion of European financial assets. Even then the ECB have stated that they may not stop there. Collectively, global QE is a breathtakingly monumental experiment by any measure and has only one stated aim and one consequence: to elevate the value of financial assets.

This is an addictive process by any measure. As we'll see, it has had unintended consequences we may have to live with for a very long time. Meanwhile the idea of QE, once an emergency policy, has been normalised in the minds of a generation. So we've had the social phenomenon called the Baby Boomers, Generation X, Generation Y, the Millennials, but are we now, in the twenty-first century, faced with Generation QE?

QE or not QE, that is the question ...

Since the millennium it hasn't been such a bad time if you were on the Forbes 500 Rich List: the total assets of the list have risen from just under a trillion dollars to just over seven trillion. That's the equivalent of an average compounded

growth rate of nearly 16% a year. There was an unfortunate dip in 2008, when the financial crisis hit, but ever since things have, if anything, accelerated. From 2009 onwards the wealth of the Forbes Rich List inhabitants increased at an annualised rate in excess of 22%. Much of it can be put down to quantitative easing combined with the effects of compounding: if you started off with anything it got bigger and at an increasing rate.

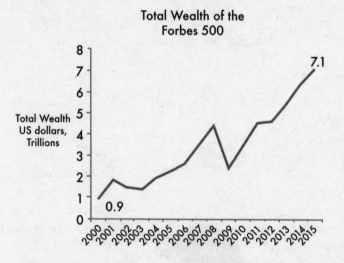

Total Wealth of the Forbes 500

QE has another aim: to offer the psychological benefit of feeling rich. Rising asset prices make people feel good – they look at their total wealth and stop fretting about their future and begin to live in the 'now'. This is the so-called 'wealth effect', which works just fine if you have any wealth. But it doesn't if you haven't.

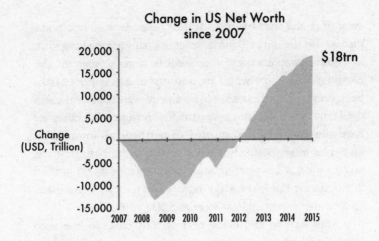

**Change in US Net Worth
since 2007**

Change
(USD, Trillion)

$18trn

20,000
15,000
10,000
5,000
0
-5,000
-10,000
-15,000

2007 2008 2009 2010 2011 2012 2013 2014 2015

The main effect of QE is to put a 'floor', or safety net, under the value of financial assets. Consequently, investors can engage in riskier and riskier activities without losing too much sleep: they know a central bank is going to be there for them if they get into trouble if market prices start to fall. This is why QE is sometimes referred to as promoting the 'moral hazard' of making money out of ever-rising markets just about a sure thing. Also, by putting a floor under markets, financial assets which may have fallen in value are falsely supported, which is a disruption of the market mechanism. To some this means the financial markets are now 'rigged' in favour of those who already have wealth.

And you have to say that, as a policy, targeting the wealth or savings of those who have financial wealth and savings QE has been overwhelmingly successful. Since the dark days of 2007 the US alone has seen its net worth – stock, bonds and real estate – rise by $18 trillion. Mark this – that's not $18 trillion from the bottom of the crisis but $18 trillion *extra* since the start of crisis. It's the equivalent of one year's income for the entire United States – a truly astonishing idea.

Some people expect there will be a reckoning for the blessings that come with QE, and just as assets prices have been pumped up there should be an equal and opposite asset deflation (price decline) as 'normality' resumes. Whether we have now entered a 'new normal' of permanently low interest rates is a moot point. But what is sure is the path that has taken us on a near-continuous journey from 3,000 BC and 20% interest rates to today's now 'close to zero' regime has created the lowest interest rates in 5,000 years.

Approaching and living permanently close to 'the zero bound' of interest rates has led some to conclude that, if we do get into trouble again, central banks will have *no alternative* but to go through the process of QE all over again. In that atmosphere 'bad news' becomes 'good news' as it signals that support mechanism will be switched on again, causing asset prices to stay high or go even higher. This sets up a very odd dynamic – something quite different from what has gone before: the market mechanism stops working, market valuations are no longer related to fundamental value while, simultaneously, increasing or maintaining the gap between the haves and the have-nots. Inequality becomes a permanent fixture of society.

I dream of Gini ...

The effect on the distribution of wealth of QE has begun to show up in official statistics. The World Bank recently released numbers on the distribution of Corrado Gini's index of income and wealth distribution. The Gini index ranges

from 1 to 100 and seeks to measure financial inequality in a society; a value of 100 means that a single person has all the money while, as it declines, money is more and more equally distributed.

Some interesting trends are showing up. For instance, in Latin America wealth inequality, although at a high level, is declining as a phenomenon. Crises like the one seen in Argentina are working to redistribute wealth while in Brazil the new-found economic prosperity is being shared by an increasingly greater proportion of society even though there is still a long way to go. Africa, notably South Africa, displays disturbingly high levels of wealth concentration in the hands of a few.

In the Gini index the UK comes out quite well with a score of just under twenty-six. In fact, equality of wealth distribution has improved markedly between 1995 and 2010 when the latest data is available and embraces the financial crisis.

The United States Gini index has shown a marked and continuous increase of inequality, something that has been occurring since the 1970s, and has accelerated as the recovery from the financial crisis has gathered pace. By 2007 the average after-tax income of the top 1% reached $1.3 million but that of the bottom 20% came to just $17,800.

QE isn't the only villain of the piece. Stagnating wages for those on low and median incomes – even if you have higher education qualifications – has become a feature of developed nations. In the US, for instance, households of individuals with bachelor's degrees or higher saw their real income fall by 10% between 2000 and 2010. Put simply, the rich are getting richer, the poor are becoming poor and more numerous while the middle class is becoming an increasing rare group.

The rich are getting richer, the poor are becoming poorer and the middle class increasingly rare...

Man vs Generation QE

I have a friend who is both a Buddhist and a psychotherapist. She leads a life of the mind, doesn't have very much regard for material possessions and by her own admission is 'happy'. I have another friend who has about £800 million in the bank, has a finger in all kinds of businesses, travels the world in his own jet and would also describe himself as 'happy'. If these two people lived in a two-person state together their happiness index would be astronomical but their Gini index would be approaching 100 and a cause for international concern. Clearly, what constitutes a happy and healthy society cannot be put down to money alone.

But there is no doubt that income and wealth inequality has risen in the first two decades of the twenty-first century; the experiences of those at the very top and very bottom of money measures have diverged markedly. Strangely, this appears to be much to do with the process of quantitative easing (combined with compound interest) as anything else. For this reason alone it is questionable that it should be habituated as a tool for a generation of decision-makers both private and public.

If at all possible, closing the inequality gap will take a very long time by natural forces alone. It may even be impossible without some form of intervention that forcibly redistributes wealth. If you wanted to put it in fancy terms you would say there needs to be a transfer of power from capital to labour. In unfancy terms, everyone needs a pay rise.

Some people say that inequality is a necessary part of a capitalist economy – it rewards those who work hard and in turn are able to engage in 'trickle-down economics', whereby the wealthy spend money which employs people who in turn spend their wages. This would be fine if it worked. In fact the opposite is true: studies show the size of the economic pie actually gets smaller as inequality increases.

Handing out more to a larger number of people makes good economic sense even if you leave aside the positive social consequences of everyone doing better and being happier. Capitalism is a process based on compounding; the more that is spent, the more is produced, which in turn means more can be spent. The best way to start the process is to put money into the hands of the many through wages. After that the virtuous circuit takes care of itself. At least that is what we can hope for; otherwise we may be stuck with Generation QE.

11

Derivatives

Where is all the money?

Have you ever wondered out loud 'Where is all the money?' If you read the financial press you could be forgiven for thinking it's locked up in the stock and bond markets. But the fact is most of the money in the world is in a place called the derivatives markets. They are simply enormous.

To put things into context, if you were to project all the money in the world onto the 102 floors of the Empire State Building it would look like this. Roughly the first eighty-one floors would be the derivatives markets. Nobody knows the exact value of the derivatives markets but some have put it as high as $1.2 quadrillion ($1.2 thousand trillion).

The next thirteen floors are occupied by the $200 trillion global debt markets. This is still large compared to the next section, the stock markets at $70 trillion (five floors), which, if you think about it, is ridiculously small compared to how much press they get. Actual notes and coins represent $29 trillion (two floors), a figure that is likely to dwindle over time as we globally embrace plastic cards but also if or when virtual currencies become popular. All the known extracted gold at $8 trillion is only slightly larger than the value of real

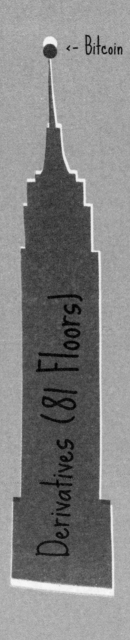
<- Bitcoin

Derivatives (81 Floors)

estate at $7 trillion (together one floor). The little red light blinking on the top is bitcoin.

So the reality is both simple and inescapable – the largest part of the global financial system in the twenty-first century is the part that most people know least about: the derivatives markets. But what are the derivatives markets? What is a derivative and how can you as a modern individual get access to them and use them?

Forward contracts

Financial derivatives are so named because their value is derived from something you don't actually own. So, for instance, you could have a derivative that mimics the movement of a stock market. The price of the derivative rises and falls just the same as the stock market but you don't own all of the underlying stocks - just the derivative.

Derivatives are astonishingly useful things because they allow investors to gain access to financial markets or protect themselves without all the meddlesome costs of owning and maintaining a complicated portfolio that requires costly administrative support. They can also be used to protect investors from volatile price movements. Derivatives provide a cheap and efficient way of gaining market exposure because:

$$Market = Cash + Derivative$$

So by having cash at the bank and owning a derivative on a market or markets (pretty much any market you can think of by the way) you can do the job of investing just as well as most professional fund managers -- if you know what you are doing that is.

By far the simplest derivative has been around since the time of the Medici, the papal bankers, in Renaissance Italy. It is a humble agreement to buy something at a fixed point in the future at a fixed price and is called a 'forward contract'. In reality we do this quite a lot although we might not realise it – it's the basis of all foreign exchange transactions, even the ones we do at the airport when we go on holiday.

Today's price is called the 'spot price' and is different from the forward price. To see why, let's use an example. Imagine you own some US dollars and want to buy some Japanese yen today and take delivery in three months' time. If you owned the US dollars *right now* you could put the dollars on deposit at the bank at an annual rate of 4.5% for three months.

$$\text{After three months} = 1,000,000 \times (1+4.5\%/4) = 1,011,250$$

'Hang on!' says the person on the other side of the transaction. 'That $11,250 should be mine!!!' 'Well, yes …' you grudgingly reply. 'But then again, I should get the interest you are receiving on the yen even if it is at a rate of 0.1% a year!!!'

You could exchange the two interest payments that you have both missed out on but there is a simpler way to achieve the same thing: adjust the price of currency by the *difference* between the two interest rates. Adding or subtracting this produces the forward price, which will be different from the spot price.

If you were to put it into a spreadsheet it would look like this:

	A	B
1	Currency (Spot) Rate	116.50
2	Time (Years)	0.25
3	Sell Interest Rate (annualised)	0.10%
4	Buy Interest (annualised)	4.50%
5	Interest Rate Difference	-4.40%
6	Time Weighted Interest Rate Difference	-1.10%
7	Future Rate	115.22

	A	B
1	Currency (Spot) Rate	116.5
2	Time (Years)	0.25
3	Sell Interest Rate (annualised)	0.001
4	Buy Interest (annualised)	0.045
5	Interest Rate Difference	=B3-B4
6	Time Weighted Interest Rate Difference	=B5*B2
7	Future Rate	=B18(1+B6)

Now, if, as it inevitably will, the yen to US dollar rate moves between now and the delivery date someone is going to be a winner and someone is going to be a loser. If you own the yen at 116.5 and it strengthens the value of the forwards, these will increase and vice versa – if the value of the yen falls, so too will the forwards. That is the foreign exchange markets – trillions of US dollars a day trade on this basis.

Forward foreign exchange contracts are fantastically flexible; you can specify any amount and any date when the parties exchange the agreed currencies. Large institutions like pension funds, banks and corporations are the main players in the forward markets as they require complex legal agreements because these are bespoke, one-to-one contracts between consenting adults. It's not the place where ordinary investors play. That's where the futures markets come in – the principles are the same but they are just a little less flexible.

Futures

The global futures market is truly impressive in its size and the breadth of things that can be bought and sold – pretty much everything from stock markets, currencies, bonds, gold, oil, metals, coffee, and my own personal favourite, lean hogs, can be traded.

The futures markets seek to reduce, among other things, the risk of your counterparty not being able to fulfil their obligations due to, say, going bust in the interim. To do this futures are traded on futures exchanges where lots of different people buy and sell. This mixing-up process of who you are trading with spreads out your exposure to any one counterparty, thereby reducing the risk of non-payment. However, it comes at a cost. To enable lots of people to trade on equal terms everything has to be standardised into tradeable bundles, which incurs a loss of flexibility. Each one of these bundles is called a 'contract'. For instance, say one

Futures = The trade of future exchanges

SPREADING THE RISK

Buy – Sell

Sell

Buy

Sell

Buy

MEANS SPREADING THE TRADES

contract is worth $100,000 of the underlying commodity. To cover $1,000,000 you would have to buy ten contracts (1,000,000/100,000). This is different from a forward where you would merely specify your desire to sell $1,000,000 of something in one go.

Another difference between forwards and futures is the delivery date. Forwards can be any business day you like: there really is no limit. But futures contracts require both parties to exchange the underlying commodity on very specific dates. They can be at the end of the month for some contracts but more usually they are at the end of each quarter year: March, June, September and December.

Living on the margin

When you buy or sell a futures contract you have to stump up some cash. This is called the *initial margin*. Each day, each second, the market is going to move and you will make or lose money on the position. The profit and loss of your position is calculated as the market varies, and if you fall into loss you will be asked to post a 'variation margin'. This is where the phrase 'margin call' comes from. Someone may call you and literally ask you for more money to cover your current losses. If you make a profit it is credited to your account.

The other thing to notice is that you have to put remarkably little down to establish quite a large position. If you were a real gambler then for just 14% of the initial value of what you are trading you could get a much higher exposure to the market. This is the essence of 'leverage'. Think about it for a moment: using the futures market you can get an exposure seven times larger than the actual amount of money you have

(1/14%) using futures. If you can see the possibilities for personal enrichment in that statement, congratulations – you have just invented the hedge fund industry.

Contracts for difference

Contracts for difference (CFDs) are the most common way to access the financial markets by individuals without actually owning anything. Like futures, they can offer a highly leveraged way of betting on the direction of the markets; they can be a route to preternatural returns and eye-watering losses. They are traded between individual traders via CFD providers. Unlike futures there are no standard contract terms for CFDs but they do tend to have some things in common.

A CFD is started by making an opening trade or 'position' via a CFD provider. There is no expiry date; all positions are left overnight and the profit or loss is credited to your account in real time. To 'close' the position, as we'll see later, you will need an equal but opposite trade; if you have bought something you have to sell it and if you have sold something you have to buy it back. Once the position is closed, the difference between the opening trade and the closing trade is paid as profit or loss, minus commissions and other costs.

Like futures, CFDs are traded on margin – you only have to put down a fraction of the notional exposure – but it also means the trader must maintain the minimum margin level at all times. If the amount of money deposited with a CFD broker drops below minimum margin level then margin calls can be made – simply, traders may need to cover their margins otherwise the CFD provider may liquidate their positions.

In practice it works like this. Let's use the US stock market index, the S&P500 which is trading at 1,900 and each CFD is worth $100. Your opening positions is worth $190,000 of which you only have to stump up 0.5% of this amount, which is a paltry $950. Now – let's start moving the market around to see what happens to the value of your position.

Opening the Position	
Buy 100 S&P500 CFDs	100 x 1,900 = $190,000
Margin requirement is 0.5% of the notional amount	190,000 x 0.005 = $950
Closing the Position	
Imagine the index has risen to 2,000	100 x 2,000 = 200,000
	Profit = 200,000 - 190,000 = $10,000
Imagine the index has fallen to 1,850	Loss = 185,000 - 190,000 = $5,000

Imagine there is great economic or company news and the stock market begins to rise to 2,000. Following the mathematics through you will make a fleeting profit of $10,000 which you can take now or continue to let it run. However, later in the afternoon, one of the largest companies in the index issues a profit warning. This leads to the market downgrading the prospects for company earnings and sends the index plunging to 1,850. You are now sitting on a $5,000 loss, which is only cushioned by the $950 you have deposited as initial margin. You now have two choices; stump up the money and run the position or enter into another transaction to sell 100 S&P500 CFDs and end this sorry affair. Strictly commissions and other costs should be taken into account, but these are small compared to the overall profit and loss. However, the principal should be clear: for a $950 down payment you could have made $10,000 (making nearly ten times your money). Conversely, you could have had a rather menacing phone call for $4,050 to cover your losses. If you don't see the financial dangers in this situation maybe derivatives aren't really for you, no matter how much you are attracted to them.

How to access the derivatives markets

It is frighteningly easy to access the derivatives markets as a private individual. The current largest ones, IG, ETX Capital, CMC Markets, Intertrader, 3D Markets, all offer a range of things you can 'bet' on including stocks, indices, currency movements and commodities like gold and oil. Execution is automatic – there is no need to talk to a dealer – and markets operate twenty-four hours a day five days a week. All you need is your initial margin, a declaration you understand the concept of leverage, you understand you can lose everything in blink of an eye, you have the wherewithal to put down your initial margin and you can afford the losses you may incur.

You could use trading accounts purely to bet on the direction of markets. Alternatively you could to create a portfolio of exposures which, when you add them all up, makes for a consistent view of the world. After all:

$$Market = Cash + Future \text{ or } CFD$$

In this case you would be buying (going 'long' as they say) the market in combination with cash to create something that moves in pretty much lock step with the actual physical market – rising and falling with it. For instance, if you had $100,000 in cash, buying futures contracts worth $100,000 or a CFD worth $100,000 would give you a very similar result to say buying every stock in the right proportion of the S&P500 index. It would be just so much easier and cheaper.

In this case we wouldn't be using the markets for supernormal profits but merely as an alternative to using the underlying assets. When your market exposure begins to exceed your cash then you are in the realms of leverage, which is, as we have seen, addictive and seductive and a dangerous place to go to as a private individual.

The other way to use a derivatives account is for 'hedging' – creating a position which offsets something else happening in your portfolio.

Say you have a stock portfolio. Using a future or CFD account, you could hedge its price movement by selling (going 'short' in the jargon) a futures or CFD contract on the market, thus turning your portolio into 'cash'. This is how it works. Rearranging our equation:

$$\text{Cash} = \text{Market} - \text{Future or CFD}$$

The negative sign indicates you are now selling the Future or CFD. 'Shorting' creates profits from falling markets in the equal and opposite way going 'long' in the market profits from rising markets. In practice this means that if the market fell, to a greater but not perfect degree, you would be protected, as the losses in the portfolio would be compensated by the profit from the short derivative position. Of course, if the market rose you would lose on the derivative position, but the gains on the rest of the portfolio would even it out. You would also need to have the cash to meet the margin call you got.

You could do this in whole or in part to protect the portfolio from downside risks if you had a view the markets may not do so well over the coming months, or say you wanted to protect the value of your portfolio because of an upcoming financial or life milestone such as retirement or the need to protect your savings because of a major purchase.

This ability to protect your wealth is why derivatives are sometimes described as 'portfolio insurance'. In this sense there is a legitimate place for derivatives in financial planning and portfolio management. The problem is, if there is a way for human beings to misuse something then they will find it and this is what gets people and institutions into the trouble if they do. After all, derivatives brought about the largest corporate loss in history when AIG, a large American insurance group, reported it lost \$61.7bn in the last quarter of 2008. The Federal Reserve had to pump \$85bn into the company to ensure the entire financial system didn't collapse. The dark side of derivatives is very dark indeed.

Man vs Derivatives

Human beings seem to be uniquely equipped to see risks both where they are and where they are not. Stan Jones isn't somebody who you might of heard of, but after this you'll probably never forget him. Stan was very worried about the run up to the year 2000 and what some thought would be the imminent demise of civilization when a well-known glitch called the Millennium Bug would bring all the computers in the world to a gear-crunching halt.

In particular, Stan was worried about the resulting lack of medication in the world when all production ceased. The chemical element silver is well known to kill bacteria and, to prepare for the bacterial outbreak to come, Stan began drinking a solution laced with the stuff. Over the years, Stan turned blue. Not a subtle blue but a Blu-Tak blue. He had become one of the few known cases of argyria. As the clocks ticked beyond midnight on New Year's Eve 1999 and nothing happened, he also became a great example of sincerely held but misplaced risk management. Fortunately, his conditions didn't stop Stan from leading an active life; he unsuccessfully ran for the US Congress - twice.

Clearly, man has a deep desire to have some kind of insurance policy - to hedge our bets to coin a phrase – and into that gap has dropped derivatives. They were specifically designed to help manage risk or as an alternative route to get market exposure, but somewhere along the road that got twisted and nearly brought down the global financial system. Given how useful they can actually be, they have had something of a bad rap in that respect.

Derivatives aren't bad per se. Some of the people who have used them have certainly abused their properties but with the ease of access to the financial markets they offer, combined with the right training and knowledge, they could become one of the most widely used areas of the market by non-professional investors in the twenty-first century.

12

Money

What is the secret of our success?

The history of mankind is the history of cooking. Ever since the day primitive man dropped a piece of meat into a fire *on purpose*, because it tasted better, we have been searching and using and incorporating extra energy to supplement our natural energy to power progress.

Using added energy is what has been behind our population growth. The physics of this is pretty straightforward: the total population of all species is limited by the available energy supply which, in the first instance, comes from the food we can scavenge. Primitive humans used about 100 watts per person when our population density on the planet was negligible. By the time we get to the industrial age we are absorbing 8,000 watts per person but there are now 400 of us crammed into each square kilometre. If it wasn't for the extra, supplemental energy we couldn't have won the mammalian population race in which we have been engaged for about a million years. Insects still have the edge over us for sheer numbers.

Stage of development	Watts used per capita	Population per square kilometre
Primitive humans	100	Very Low
Hunter-gatherer	300	0.06
Agricultural	2,000	40
Industrial	8,000	400

Gathering your own 'extra' energy gives you an edge, extending your range to the point where you can survive in places in which you might not otherwise have done: think of an explorer huddling around a gas stove in the middle of the Arctic and you get the right mental picture. It also frees you up to do other things like develop your brain, leading to sophisticated language, science and culture. Cooking was only the first step on the journey: Karl Marx noted that metallurgy is the true sign of a civilised society. Making metals requires huge amounts of energy. The whole process of adding energy has been transformative for the human race.

Humans being humans, this wasn't enough for us and, to throw gasoline onto this already roaring fire, we added in debt. Adding debt leverages up the system and once it gets going it is pretty much unstoppable. If you wanted to put the secret of our success into an equation it would look something like this:

$$\text{Human Success} = \text{Natural Energy} + \text{Supplementary Energy} + \text{Debt}$$

What's obvious from this equation is that our economic success is very much related to our continuous expansion of energy usage and building up more and more debt. The big questions of the twenty-first century are whether we are nearing the limits of the economics that have, so far, sponsored our success, and does this mean we will reach our economic peak in the twenty-first century?

Energy and inflation

Economic growth is synonymous with energy usage: as global economic growth has increased so has our energy consumption. But, just as the drag of a car builds up rapidly as its speed increases, requiring more and more horsepower to move it 1mph faster as you go up the scale, so it is with the global economy: as the global economy becomes larger it requires a higher rate of energy usage to move the same distance as before. Over time, your need for and dependency on increasing amounts of energy becomes increasingly and dangerously unstable.

We've seen examples of this in the past. The most notorious moments of economic instability related to energy were the two so-called 'oil shocks' of the 1970s. The first occurred in 1973 when members of the Organization of Arab Petroleum Exporting Countries (OPEC) imposed an embargo on exporting oil as a protest against American

involvement in the Yom Kippur War. The price of oil rose rapidly from $3 to $12 a barrel – a fourfold increase. The second oil shock came as a result of revolution in Iran in 1979. This time oil rose from about $16 a barrel to nearly $40. On both occasions the net result, for the world, was a period of cripplingly high inflation, recession and unemployment.

Despite these events we have consistently pursued economic growth built upon fossil fuels, albeit that there is now an awareness that this is not a sustainable policy: one day, everything commercially viable to extract will have been extracted. We would then start to deplete the world's reserves. From this peak, the clock would begin ticking on our carbon-based society. This is the idea around 'peak oil'.

The onset or approach to 'peak oil', the point at which we start to run out of exploitable oil, has been a controversial and surprisingly old topic: it was first debated as long ago as 1906. Since then the peak has proved to be something of a moveable feast. Some say we have passed peak oil production; others believe this to be somewhat alarmist. The latest estimates converge on oil production peaking somewhere between 2020 and 2030. Peak oil is most definitely a twenty-first-century problem and marks the bursting of the carbon-rich bubble we have lived in for some three hundred years.

Whatever the truth of the exact time our oil reserves will begin to dwindle, the one thing most experts have long agreed upon is, way before we find viable substitutes the price of oil will rocket, bringing with it a 1970s-style inflationary shock to the global economy. As Lord Oxburgh, a former chairman of the oil giant Shell, said in 2008, 'It is pretty clear that there is not much chance of finding any significant quantity of new cheap oil. Any new or unconventional oil is going to be expensive.' Clearly, the days of sticking a pickaxe into the ground and seeing crude oil bubbling to the surface are long gone. There are now oil explorers looking to drill down 30,000 feet into the ocean just to find out there isn't anything there.

An inflationary shock of this sort would, as it did in the 1970s, have profound effects on society: on wages, interest rate policy, government spending, consumer spending, currency values, bond yields and the level of the stock markets. More to point, all these things impact upon all of us directly and indirectly in our personal and professional lives: the price of food, the cost of filling up our car and our monthly mortgage payments (to name but a few) will all be affected. Or, as the 2005 United States Department of Energy Hirsch Report put it, '… without timely mitigation, the economic, social, and political costs [of peak oil] will be unprecedented. Viable mitigation options exist on both the supply and demand sides, but to have substantial impact, they must be initiated more than a decade in advance of peaking.'

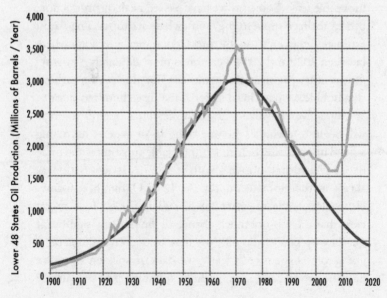

More recently the picture has become somewhat confusing. The most accurate peak oil model produced by geologist

M. King Hubbert was progressing unnervingly accurately: the peak production for oil was achieved in 1970, following which it began to decline in a steady manner until we got to 2010. The world then went into a phase of massive oil over-production principally through the use of 'new' sources of oil from shale, oil sands and other conversion processes which has helped oil prices collapse from over $100 a barrel to $30. In the short term this has contributed to a period of low inflation, and the idea that we can push back the end of our relationship with oil, but the fact remains that we are still living in a carbon-based society and in the next phase of our development we will use more oil than has so far been used in the entire history of mankind.

By some estimates, renewable sources of energy still contribute relatively little to the overall energy consumption of the world: it has been estimated that only approximately 11% of the world's energy comes in this form, rising to 15% by 2040. Others are more optimistic. According to a 2011 projection by the International Energy Agency, solar power generators may produce most of the world's electricity within fifty years, reducing the emission of greenhouse gases harming the environment while significantly reducing our dependency on oil. However, this is not to say there won't be a painful transition in the interim; allowing the markets to dictate when alternative sources of energy become viable will see conventional energy prices rise long before the necessary innovation has been perfected.

Debt

In the so-called developed economies we have been playing a capitalist game for over 150 years with some intensity but also with some restraint. Things really took off in the 1980s when personal credit was extended through the availability of credit cards, personal loans and the idea that homeownership should be a universal aspiration. The growth in borrowed money exploded as we pursued the idea that we could all be equal in our material possessions as long as we travelled in the vehicle of debt. This paused for a moment when the credit crunch arrived in 2007 but, having gathered our collective breath, we started the process all over again.

The credit crunch also saw many governments expand their debt levels and, as we have seen in previous chapters, many developed countries have debt/income ratios approaching or over 100%. This process of personal and government debt expansion can go on for a considerable time but one day the cost may well be major currency devaluations combined with

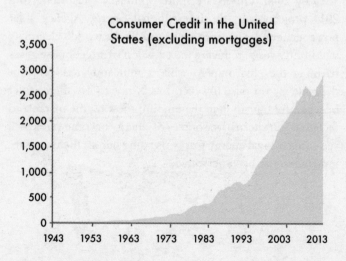

Consumer Credit in the United States (excluding mortgages)

defaults by developed nations, something unthinkable in the early twenty-first century.

This is in stark contrast to other so-called Emerging Nations. Whereas the developed nations have run deficits, the developing nations have cash in the bank. China has nearly $4 trillion in its bank account while Russia, India and Brazil have more than $350 billion each.

This is a new dynamic in the twenty-first century: debt-laden developed economies competing with relatively debt-free economies which have aspirations to emulate their living standards that are visible, so far, only from a distance. However, this also means the thing that turbocharged our development (debt) may be about to be switched off or at least turned down, leading to a slowing down (if not a cessation) of the path of continuous growth we have experienced for thousands of years.

Man vs The Planet

In the past century and a half, leaving aside one-off shocks, the global economy has grown by 2–3% every year. It's been pretty impressive and lifted vast swathes of humanity out of subsistence and into affluence, sometimes whether they wanted it or not. But they say whatever is your strength eventually becomes your weakness. Our strengths have certainly been our ingenious use of supplemental energy and debt.

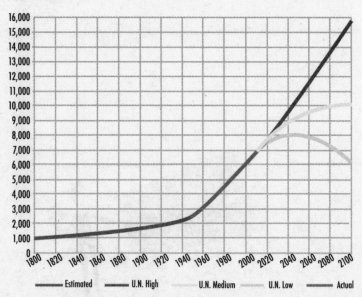

The continuing dominance of the human race on earth has been intimately linked with getting hold of more and more energy and the expansion of debt. However, there can only be so much debt a civilisation can take on before the process peaks or goes into reverse.

This has led some to conclude that there is a limit to the size of the global economy and with it the human population. This may well be our greatest challenge in the remainder of the twenty-first century; ultimately it may limit how many human beings will inhabit the earth.

According to a United Nations model of population growth this was beginning to happen in any case: by their estimates, the global population tops out at about eight billion people in 2045. Unless we expand GDP per person as the peak is passed, global GDP will start to decline naturally and the twenty-first century may be seen as the peak of our existence.

Afterword

Our relationship with money is clearly changing. Not long from now we could expect to be crowdfunding bitcoins on our internet-enabled smart watches for our new web-based global micro-venture as we glide along in one-piece jumpsuits on conveyor belts concealed in a climate-controlled bubble towards yet another leisure activity. Either that or we will continue to be packed like sardines into public transport as we trundle to a job that barely pays the mortgage and pray every night interest rates never rise lest our financial world collapse. It is for you to decide which is the more likely.

Fortunately, the world only ends once: we have a terrible tendency when it comes to money, its creation, preservation or destruction, of seeing catastrophes where they could be but most likely aren't. It's part of the curse of money. However, it must be admitted, from time to time, things do go badly wrong, which merely adds to our anxiety. On the plus side, mankind has a seemingly limitless capacity to pull itself back from the brink, waving its arms with just sufficient centrifugal force so as to stop itself from falling over the cliff. There is no reason to believe this won't be the case in the future.

In the meantime, it is inescapably true that the so-called developed markets have become just a little too intimate with money in the twentieth century. We crave it and have used it as a means to make us all appear equivalent, if only in a material sense, as long as we have been prepared to travel in the vehicle of debt to get it. It is only the extent to which we are indebted that differentiates us.

Fortunately, there is help at hand in the shape of the Emerging Markets, a group who have had only a walk-on part so far. Whereas we have debt, the Emerging Nations have money. Lots of it. But, until now, the developing nations have been able to assume access to this wealth as a cheap source of funding. As the century progresses, the competition for the available funds is increasing. The profit motive will never be vanquished from the narrative of money but what is blossoming is a new set of values pushing global companies towards policies that:

- Promote sustainability
- Value long-term investment over short-term gratification
- Share profits more evenly between capital and labour
- Spread wealth more evenly over the planet

The 'cost' may well be a less fuel-injected, turbo-driven, and yes even more boring economics, but one which not so much banishes the ups and downs of the economic cycle but at least calms it down a bit. It may well be a price worth paying. Without it there could be quite a lot of arm-waving on tiptoes to be done in the twenty-first century.

Notes

p. 20   The market price will sink …: *The Wealth of Nations*, Chapter 7.

p. 37   compared to 1,596: http://http://news.nationalgeographic.com/
news/2015/03/150302-giant-pandas-animals-science-conservation-china/

p. 46   the genuine progress indicator: Marc Miringoff and Marque-Luisa Miringoff, *The Social Health of the Nation: How America is Really Doing*, Oxford University Press, 1999.

p. 47   providing meals in elementary schools: Taken from US GDP statistics for Q2 2015, BEA.

p. 61   'Compound interest.': http://skeptics.stackexchange.com/questions/25330/did-einstein-ever-remark-on-compound-interest/25331

p. 71   was nearly $40 trillion: SIFMA, Q1 2015.

p. 71   top five hundred companies: Based on today's value of the S&P500.

p. 71   and it's rising every day: Data source: Bloomberg WDCM screen September 2015.

p. 72   global bonds are traded each day: http://www.statista.com/statistics/247092/
transaction-volume-of-debt-securities-on-the-global-bond-market/; http://www.
statista.com/statistics/189302/trading-volume-of-us-treasury-securities-since-1990/

p. 77   25% on your original investment: You won't be able to work this out using the equation here. Also you'll notice that the price movement for the same yield movement up and down isn't symmetrical: it rises by $39 but falls by $25 when interest rates are moving 2% either side of the starting point. There is a good reason for this but it's outside the scope of this book. The main point is to note the direction not the magnitude of the move for now.

p. 83   flowed into bond funds alone: http://www.icifactbook.org/fb_ch2.html

p. 90   people called 'rate tarts': You'll notice that a banker seeking the highest rate of return is called 'a consummate professional who optimises the rate of return of capital deployed' while a client who does the same thing is called 'a rate tart' …

p. 92   lending out customers' deposits: https://www.imf.org/External/Pubs/FT/
GFSR/2013/02/pdf/c3.pdf

p. 92   in various guises: https://www.imf.org/External/Pubs/FT/GFSR/2013/02/pdf/
c3.pdf

p. 95   the risks are higher: https://www.imf.org/External/Pubs/FT/GFSR/2013/02/pdf/
c3.pdf

p. 95   heading for trouble: http://www.bankofengland.co.uk/publications/Documents/
quarterlybulletin/2014/qb14q402.pdf

p. 98   Being in banking is a great life: https://en.wikipedia.org/wiki/Capital_adequacy_ratio

p. 103   to 950% of GDP: http://www.bankofengland.co.uk/publications/Documents/
quarterlybulletin/2014/qb14q402.pdf

p. 109   its own mystical language: http://www.bloomberg.com/news/articles/2015-10-11/
china-stock-rally-to-rout-about-to-repeat-for-chartist-schroeder

p. 111   having any real meaning: It could, of course, be the case that the algorithm for generating random numbers isn't as random as it likes to think it is but if you want to go there we really are disappearing down the rabbit hole.

p. 111   in a field late at night: Pearson, K. and Rayleigh, Lord (1905), 'The Problem of the Random Walk in Nature', *Nature*, Vol. 72, pp. 294, 318, 342.

p. 113   followed by higher returns: Terence C. Mills, 'Predicting the Unpredictable?', p, 29. Institute of Economic Affairs, Occasional Paper 87.

p. 118   the entire city of New York: https://www.ted.com/talks/kevin_slavin_how_algorithms_shape_our_world?language=en#t-708415

p. 125   a hole in the middle: McManus, Lori, *Money through History* (Understanding Money). Chicago, IL: Heinemann Library, 2012.

p. 131   three ways to use your coins: http://www.coindesk.com/information/sell-bitcoin/

p. 135   you guessed it, bitcoin: http://krebsonsecurity.com/2015/10/talktalk-hackers-demanded-80k-in-bitcoin/

p. 137   its true value is zero: Quiggin, John (16 April 2013). 'The Bitcoin Bubble and a Bad Hypothesis', The National Interest. Retrieved 31 October 2014.

p. 137   a value of $40,000: Schroeder, Stan (1 December 2013), 'Cameron Winklevoss: Bitcoin Might Hit $40,000 Per Coin', Mashable (New York). Retrieved 31 October 2014.

p. 138   they invested just £2 billion: http://www.vox.com/technology/2015/10/31/9651168/bitcoin-growing

p. 144   paying the money back: http://www.vanityfair.com/news/2010/10/greeks-bearing-bonds-201010

p. 144   since the 1980s: https://en.wikipedia.org/wiki/Sovereign_default

p. 160   are surprisingly uniform: https://en.wikipedia.org/wiki/List_of_countries_by_tax_rates

p. 161   the weight of $640 million: https://en.wikipedia.org/wiki/Millionaire

p. 162   above $5 million: UBS study reported in http://www.dailymail.co.uk/news/article-2380376/Thats-bit-rich-Only-28-cent-millionaires-think-theyre-wealthy.html

p. 164   difficult to comprehend: Much of the information is from http://www.forbes.com/sites/chasewithorn/2015/03/02/forbes-billionaires-full-list-of-the-500-richest-people-in-the-world-2015/

p. 164   the Forbes 500 Rich List: https://en.wikipedia.org/wiki/The_World%27s_Billionaires#2000

p. 167   with less than $1 billion: http://stats.areppim.com/listes/list_billionairesx00xwor.htm

p. 168   world record Powerball win: https://en.wikipedia.org/wiki/Lottery_jackpot_records

p. 178   lowest interest rates in 5,000 years: http://uk.businessinsider.com/chart-5000-years-of-interest-rates-2015-9?r=US&IR=T

p. 180   came to just $17,800: Stiglitz, J.E., *The Price of Inequality*, W.W. Norton. 2012, Chapter 1, p. 5

p. 180   between 2000 and 2010: http://www.census.gov/hhes/www/income/data/historical/household

p. 183   In fact the opposite is true: Stiglitz, J.E., *The Price of Inequality*, Chapter 1, p. 8.

p. 189   blinking on the top is bitcoin: http://www.valuewalk.com/wp-content/uploads/2015/12/All-Of-The-Worlds-Money-And-Markets-In-One-Visualization-Infographic.png

p. 192   **that can be traded**: 'Liquidity Pyramid', Independent Research, 10 March 2006.

p. 205   **is pretty straightforward**: http://ourfiniteworld.com/2015/05/06/why-we-have-an-oversupply-of-almost-everything-oil-labor-capital-etc/

p. 206   **Stage of development**: 'The Metabolism of a Human-Dominant Planet', in Goldin, Ian, ed., *Is the Planet Full?*, Oxford University Press, 2014.

p. 209   **oil is going to be expensive**: https://en.wikipedia.org/wiki/Peak_oil

p. 210   **Department of Energy Hirsch Report**: Hirsch, Robert L., Bezdek, Roger and Wendling, Robert (February 2005), 'Peaking of World Oil Production: Impacts, Mitigation, & Risk Management'. Science Applications International Corporation.

p. 211   **comes in this form**: http://www.eia.gov/tools/faqs/faq.cfm?id=527&t=1

p. 211   **harming the environment**: https://en.wikipedia.org/wiki/Renewable_energy

p. 213   **more than $350 billion**: https://en.wikipedia.org/wiki/List_of_countries_by_foreign-exchange_reserves

Acknowledgements

Among the many people to whom I am indebted for assistance and encouragement during the preparation of this book, I would especially like to thank Diane Weitz, aunt of my kind and patient commissioning editor (whose idea *Man vs Money* was) Lucy Warburton. It was Diane who brought us together by a route so circuitous it deserves a book in and of itself. But above all, I would like to thank my long-suffering family: wife Alice and children Alex, Georgia and Phoebe, who have had to endure the spectacle of my pacing my garden office late at night all these months muttering to myself and waving my arms furiously as I tried to explain this curious world of money, mainly to myself.

Index